The Story of WSFS into the 21ˢᵗ Century

The Path to Sustained Excellence

STRATEGY, CULTURE AND TEAM

MARK A. TURNER
BRITTANY KRIEGSTEIN
and LIZZIE SIMON

ISBN: 978-8-9922598-1-0 (E-book)
ISBN: 978-8-9922598-0-3 (Hardcover)

Book Design by *the*BookDesigners, Alan Dino Hebel & Ian Koviak

Published by Pathways Publishing in the United States of America.

Advance Praise for
The Path to Sustained Excellence

Mark Turner and associates offer a compelling, close-in account of how to build a company dozens of times faster than its competitors through a combination of culture and character. For getting going and moving fast, here is the instructor's manual for principled growth. With gripping insider accounts of everything from CEO sabbaticals to crisis comebacks, *The Path to Sustained Excellence* is a driver's manual for taking charge and leading change when it really counts.

—**Michael Useem,** faculty director of the McNulty Leadership Program, The Wharton School at the University of Pennsylvania; author of *The Edge: How 10 CEOs Learned to Lead*

In a turbulent world, *The Path to Sustained Excellence* is a vivid, engaging, and inspiring story of leadership in action. I highly recommend this exceptional book to everyone running, or looking to run an organization—you will come away with actionable, invaluable insights for the present moment and for years to come.

—**Ram Charan,** author of 36 books including *The New York Times* best-seller, *Execution*

Once I started reading *The Path to Sustained Excellence*, I could not put it down. I highly recommend it, not just for WSFS' inspiring journey, but for the book's very practical advice for those who truly want to succeed in business and make a difference.

—**Raj Gupta,** former CEO/chair of multiple Fortune 500 companies; author of *Eight Dollars and a Dream*

Mark Turner is a "master leader" who transformed WSFS Bank from a small player in the banking capital of the nation to a formidable competitor amongst all the majors. His "secret sauce" for success is shared with those who hold this book, including extraordinary lessons for others to follow by way of technology, customer centricity; and even a unique and incredibly insightful innovation in selecting his own successor. The book is a must-read for any leader who wants to shift the gears of corporate performance up a few notches, and enhance TSR.

—**Dennis Carey,** vice chair, Korn Ferry; author of *Boards That Lead* and *Talent, Strategy, and Risk*

The Path to Sustained Excellence stands as a masterclass in value creation through organizational transformation, written with the precision of a journalist and the heart of a leader. The book stands as much more than a recounting of achievements; it is a blueprint for navigating complexity and creating strategic clarity told from a deeply human perspective. Aspiring leaders and seasoned executives will all find in these pages actionable lessons that resonate far beyond WSFS Bank and the banking industry.

—**Dr. Jeff Klein,** executive director, McNulty Leadership Program, The Wharton School

The story of WSFS looks a lot like Mark Turner's personal story. Both had to scrap their way to the top, overcoming plenty of challenges along the way. This is an inspiring and enjoyable read about an important Delaware institution, and a leader who contributed so much; not just to his bank, but to his state.

—**the Honorable Jack Markell,** former governor of Delaware

In *The Path to Sustained Excellence*, Mark Turner pulls back the curtain to show how a challenged local company was transformed into a premier, national institution—using strategy, innovation, morale, expansion, teamwork, and governance; and by overcoming personal challenges. It's a powerful read.

—**Rusty Conner III,** senior partner, Covington & Burling LLP;
former rector, University of Virginia

Full of nuggets of wisdom from a long and illustrious career, *The Path to Sustained Excellence* is so much more engaging, and more personal, than I expected it to be. It's a "must read" for those who stand to learn from Mark and WSFS' scars and successes.

—**Anat Bird,** CEO, SuperCommunity Bank Forums; former bank executive

As you'll see in *The Path to Sustained Excellence*, Mark is one of those rare leaders who has real vision, and knows how to execute on it. He has done a tremendous job growing WSFS from a small community bank into one of the most well-respected regional banks in the nation. His leadership and ability to connect with people is what sets him apart from the rest.

—**Jimmy Dunne,** vice chair and senior managing principal of
Piper Sandler & Co.

Retrofitting a culture is perhaps the most difficult thing to do in business. The team at WSFS did it ... and I got to witness it first hand. *The Path to Sustained Excellence* captures the big moves, the team building and the personal sacrifices that drove a near-broken bank on its journey to greatness.

—**Ted Weschler,** investment manager, Berkshire Hathaway Inc.

TABLE OF CONTENTS

Every cloud has a silver lining;
if you can't see it, find it;
if you can't find it, make it.

—Mark A. Turner,
with apologies to John Milton

PREFACE

By Mark Turner

One evening in the early months of the Great Recession, when the world seemed awash in despair and each day seemed to unravel with chaos, I found myself drawn to a large, commanding portrait of Frederick Stone in our executive lobby.

Mr. Stone had been the president of Wilmington Savings Fund Society (WSFS Bank) from 1917 to 1954, and his look seemed to pierce through the upheavals he navigated—World War I, the Great Depression, World War II, the Cold War, and the Korean War. How, I wondered, had he managed?

I was 45 at the time, new in the role of CEO, and grappling with the aftermath of the worst financial crisis and economy in almost 80 years. We were now faced with the daunting questions of how the banking system and WSFS would withstand the strain. The weight of leading the bank—a venerable institution with a legacy spanning 176 years—and a vast network of thousands of employees, clients, investors, and partners was immense.

My anxiety was intense, and insomnia had set in, making each step forward an exercise in will. A natural introvert, I had always internalized stress. When I was young, it manifested with headaches;

and, in adulthood, stress coalesced into back pain, ulcers, and sleep problems. Now the stress was debilitating, and because I was CEO, it was challenging the future of the entire organization.

Still, as I stared at Frederick Stone's portrait, I heard myself saying: "If he could do *that*, we can do *this*."

Ultimately, during my time at WSFS, we created the kind of success I never would have imagined. Sometimes we simplify it with the quip "10 times, 20 times, 30 times" (aka, "10, 20, 30"): In the space of my 25 years at the bank, we grew about 10 times in asset size, about 20 times in revenue and profit, and about 30 times in value. We guided WSFS from a market value of approximately $100 million, to over $3 billion on the NASDAQ exchange, outperforming the shareholder returns of peers and broader indexes by a factor of many times. But the numbers alone fail to capture the essence of the journey: the risks taken, the obstacles overcome, the big wins, the lessons learned; and, most importantly, the people who made our success possible. With the clarity of time, I realized that I had a lot more to share than the end result of our company's financial achievements. In the pages to follow, I will discuss how that success was achieved through the steadfast commitment to strategy, culture, and team.

The 2008 financial crisis and the Great Recession, with their persistent aftershocks, tested every business and leader as we scrambled to sustain our institutions and restore public trust. Yet many of the most harrowing experiences I faced were deeply personal, brought on by my fear of not measuring up, and through self-neglect. There were moments when I nearly lost my bearings, risking my health and the trust of those I cherished. Confronting these dark episodes, seeking professional help and the help of colleagues and loved ones—and eventually overcoming the challenges—made me a better leader, husband, father, and friend. In sharing these aspects of my journey, I hope to inspire others to seek the support of confidants, and take care of their own physical and mental health during their ambitious and trying professional years. I believe that while our successes might impress you, my stumbles have something more meaningful to offer.

We also wanted the book to reflect the deep reverence we have for teamwork. There will be recollections and reflections from some of the key people who gave WSFS everything they had over the course of those 25 years, resulting in that incredible "10, 20, 30." Journalist Brittany Kriegstein, one of my co-writers, has interviewed former CEO Skip Schoenhals, Chief Human Capital Officer Peggy Eddens, COO Karl Johnston, former board member Ted Weschler, and many others who provided invaluable perspectives. Their voices will illuminate various events at the bank through their own vantage points. Likewise, current CEO Rodger Levenson will offer insights into his rise, and into WSFS today. Finally, the Appendix will house essential strategies, lessons, and advice learned through experiences, both good and bad.

Where It Started

To understand how I arrived at WSFS, it's helpful to trace my roots. I was born in 1963, the second-to-last of nine children to John "Jack" Turner and Helen (née Katulka) Turner. We lived on the first floor of a two-story brick row home in North Philadelphia, near North 5th Street and Lehigh Avenue. My mother, a strong Catholic woman with Eastern European heritage, held the family together with my father, also a Catholic, and of Irish descent. Together, they represented the archetype of conscientious, lower-middle-class Americans of the Traditionalist Generation, a demographic that filled our neighborhoods.

When I was three, we moved back to the Logan section of North Philly, where my dad's family had roots spanning three generations. Our home on the 5300 block of Camac Street was very modest—three small bedrooms and one bathroom for 11 people and a dog—but it was the center of an increasingly diverse, vibrant neighborhood. My siblings and I would tumble into the streets and alleyways, joining up with other kids in games common to inner-city streets. We didn't need much—just a ball, some chalk, and a bit of creativity. We played all sorts of games: chase, red rover, hot beans, doorbell dixie, bottlecaps, wall ball, step ball, roof ball, wire ball, handball, and half ball. The most versatile play implement was a pimple ball—thirty-five cents, rubbery, and textured—that still evokes fond memories of my childhood.

Life wasn't all fun and games, though. Being diligent in school was a must, as was completing daily house chores. Money was tight. Meals were basic: grilled cheese, meatloaf, liver and onions, peas and green beans, and always some form of potato. We wore hand-me-downs until our teenage years. There was no allowance. If you wanted a candy bar or a soda, you had to work for it. In the afternoons, we would grab a buddy and offer to bag groceries, or sweep stoops and sidewalks, for a quarter. We'd wake up early to shovel sidewalks, cut grass, or deliver newspapers. We became scrappy little entrepreneurs, finding ways to make our own money.

With a large circle of friends came a multitude of supportive parents. Every block had adults who would watch us, feed us, and mend our scrapes. When it was time to settle down, we'd gather on porches to play card games like pinochle, or board games like Risk, and only when the streetlights flickered on would we head home. This close-knit community was my first taste of what I now think of as "culture"—a shared sense of pride, expected behaviors, and mutual support that would later shape my approach at WSFS.

This tight-knit neighborhood wasn't just a boon for us kids, it was vital for our hardworking parents. My mom handled most of the many parental house duties and dad juggled multiple jobs to support us financially—selling life insurance by day; bartending at Charlie's, the corner bar, by night; and working weekends for a catering company. When my younger brother and I were nine and 10 years old—old enough not to burn the house down—my mom went back to work: first as a secretary at Philadelphia High School for Girls, and then for Blue Cross Blue Shield. With both parents working long hours, we had to be pretty self-sufficient, and also depend on our older siblings and neighbors for care.

Despite time and financial constraints, my parents focused on four essential things: a roof over our heads, clothes on our backs, food on the table, and, importantly, the best education they could afford. Dissatisfied with local public schools, they made sacrifices to send us to Catholic schools—a world of uniforms and discipline. It was a stretch, but their commitment never wavered. They embodied a "whatever it takes" mindset that I've always remembered and tried to emulate.

My strong educational foundation paid off when I secured a partial scholarship to St. Joseph's Preparatory School, which was one of the city's foremost high schools. It was at "The Prep" where my academic and personal development truly began to flourish. Under the inspiration of my older brother Timmy and great friend Tim Barton, I immersed myself in track and cross country, disciplines that became more than mere sport, as I lacked the innate talent that many of my teammates possessed. Only my dogged dedication could distinguish me. And each grueling team practice, each solitary run through the pain and fatigue, sculpted a framework of determination and resilience within me. This rigorous regimen—getting out there every day, sometimes twice a day; regardless of place, time, and conditions; pushing through physical and mental barriers—instilled virtues of discipline, perseverance, and tenacity that would become the bedrock of my professional life. When you've gone out there and done it, you're glad you did. That was something that would stick with me throughout my career. No one ever felt worse after a good run, or a hard day's work.

By the time senior year arrived, our family had moved out of North Philly, which meant a two-hour trek each way on public transit to reach The Prep. Starting in the morning dark, I took the bus, the elevated train (The "L"), and then the trolley across Girard Avenue. After school and practice, I did the same in reverse, arriving home in the evening dark. It was a challenge, but I had no choice: I had to persevere through the long days. I was admitted to a good private college in Erie, Pennsylvania, but when registration time came, my parents realized that we didn't have the money to send me there. It was July of 1981, and the economy wasn't doing well.

So, I recalibrated and chose La Salle University, which had a good reputation and a modest tuition. Critically, I could commute; it was ironically right back in our old North Philly neighborhood, and a school where both my dad and older brother had attended. I took out loans; applied for small scholarships; and worked nights, weekends, holidays, and summers to pay for school. Like my commute to The Prep, my commute to La Salle wasn't easy; it required navigating three different buses each way, totaling, again, four hours of travel per day. But I put my head down and made it work. It was at La Salle where the pieces fell into place. I met Regina, who would become my wife and partner for the next 40 years and counting, and Steve Booth, who became my best man and lifelong friend. In retrospect, every twist and turn served a greater purpose. I wouldn't trade my journey for anything.

By junior year, I scraped together enough money to rent an apartment near campus with Steve. As I considered my major, I looked to my older siblings, many of whom had degrees in the humanities—English, psychology, philosophy, and other subjects that became popular in the '60s and '70s. But after graduation, some were struggling with job prospects. I decided to enroll in La Salle's business school, studying accounting and management, choosing a path with clearer job prospects. After that, I planned to take life as it came.

The Working World

Graduating near the top of my class from La Salle, I joined global professional services firm Peat, Marwick & Mitchell (which, in 1987, became KPMG). I was well trained, worked extremely hard, and received help from some key role models, like John Broderick, partner. But after almost eight years in the "Big 8,"

I wanted more. To me, it felt like accounting and auditing were all about looking into the past; I was more interested in creating value for the future.

Banking became the answer. In the early '90s, I joined the Corporate Development department of Meridian Bank in Reading, Pennsylvania. It was mostly mergers and acquisitions (M&A), and I loved it. I had a disciplined and great boss in Mike Hughes, who gave me a functional MBA in finance and banking. Meridian's small scale offered significant responsibility, but its subsequent sale to CoreStates Bank, a much larger entity, made me feel like a mere cog in the machine. I could have worked 24/7, or not come in at all, and neither would have mattered. I wanted to make a difference.

Here's where WSFS comes in. At the time, it was a community bank that was coming off a very rough stretch—almost failing a few years before I joined, and still struggling. But it had new, strong leadership, and there seemed to be many opportunities to make an impact.

The rest of the story will follow, of course. But I think those lessons I learned as an inner-city Philly kid—the hard work, the perseverance, the self-starting, the personal responsibility, the community-building skills—eventually served me well as I led WSFS. When the going got tough, I just kept going, as my parents did, waking up each morning committed to do *whatever it takes* to move things forward.

My parents were proud to see my career progress, particularly when WSFS sponsored my MBA from The Wharton School at the University of Pennsylvania, and when I was named CEO. Driving down I-95 on the way to the beach, they always looked forward to passing Wilmington, where they'd catch a glimpse of the massive green W-S-F-S on top of the bank's headquarters.

They're both gone now. My mom and dad passed comfortably, surrounded by the loving, tight-knit family they'd worked so hard to raise. I know we've all gone on to honor their legacies in meaningful ways.

Hard work, discipline, and my willingness to struggle and keep going, took me further in life than I ever imagined I'd go.

But personal grit could only take me so far. To get to the peak of my own capacity, and to bring WSFS from good to truly great, required a dedication to collaborative efforts. Our biggest gains—and our escape from our biggest losses—came from a steadfast, multi-year commitment to strategy, culture, and team: together, they are the path to sustained excellence.

ONE | A ROUGH START

By Mark Turner

By 1996, the Wilmington Savings Fund Society had weathered its fair share of storms. Through depressions, wars, social upheavals, widespread bank failures, and the occasional internal crisis, the thrift had managed to endure 164 years. This resilience was a testament to the many generations of leaders who had left their mark on the institution. But by this point, the existential crisis of the early 1990s had passed, WSFS was trading in the market at values well above its lows, and the idea of selling the bank was under serious consideration by the board and investors who put down money in the dark days.

March of that year would prove to be a pivotal month that would change everything. Marvin "Skip" Schoenhals, the CEO at the time, along with the board and big investors Ted Weschler and John Rollins, made a game-changing decision: after running a public auction process, they opted against selling the bank. This was not just a business decision; it was a declaration of independence. Skip's vision was clear: he wanted to lay the groundwork for WSFS' long-term success. However, the looming threat of a sale had driven away some of the bank's most talented individuals. To secure the future, Skip needed to bring in a new generation of leaders, a cadre of fresh talent to guide the bank into its next phase.

Right away, he needed to fill four crucial roles: WSFS needed a new head of retail banking, a head of commercial banking, a chief technology officer, and a controller who might ultimately succeed Bill Abbott, the bank's CFO. It was time to start searching.

Here's where I come into the picture. At 33, I had spent three years as vice president of finance at Meridian Bank in Reading, Pennsylvania, a bank recently absorbed by CoreStates Bank. In the grand merger play, I had become just another face in a sprawling corporate behemoth. Despite the prestige of CoreStates—at the time, one of the top 20 banks in the country—I had become one of 20,000 employees, and on the outer edges of the organization. It was clear: no matter how hard I worked, I'd never make a real impact there. So, I began my search for a new role, where my contributions would be more significant. A few colleagues from KPMG, the accounting firm where I had cut my teeth, including Dave Reavy and John Depman who knew me well, pointed me towards WSFS.

Their pitch was enticing: *Here's an organization needing more strong leadership at a critical juncture. This is a place where you can make a real difference.*

I applied, and soon found myself subjected to a rigorous vetting process. Psychologists analyzed me; senior bank officials interrogated me. Yet, it was my interactions with Skip Schoenhals and Bill Abbott that left the deepest impression. Their wisdom, integrity, and vision were palpable, and I was excited by the idea of joining their ranks.

I pursued the job all the way until they made me an offer, but then I hesitated. Having recently been through two mergers where my employers were sold out from under me, I was wary. I feared the same fate might await me at WSFS, so I turned down the position. Bill, crestfallen by my refusal, insisted on another meeting.

I thought about it and decided to go. When I returned to his office, he shared something new with me. "I'm 56," he said, "and I only want to work till I'm 58. If you prove yourself, there's a real chance you could become CFO while still relatively young." That was compelling, but it was Skip's resolute promise that clinched it for me. He looked me squarely in the eye and said, "I'm not selling this bank."

That pointed commitment to independence convinced me to accept the offer.

On August 12, 1996, I started at WSFS as the controller. In that year's annual report, Skip introduced me alongside two other recent hires: Chief Information Officer Tom Stevenson, and Executive Vice President of Retail Banking Joe Murphy. Our team's collective experience—over 200 years in financial institutions—was impressive.

My initial focus was on internal and external accounting— ensuring records were accurate, payments were processed correctly, and essential information was communicated effectively. Despite Skip's efforts, the bank still had ghosts from its past: bad real estate loans, and failed ventures. While this wasn't nearly as dire as the bank's previous struggles, cleaning them up was crucial for WSFS' transformation.

Fortunately, we had help. WSFS had brought in Sheshunoff, a consulting firm specializing in re-engineering to streamline operations and cut costs. When I stepped into the middle of that process, it was very clear that the company had a long way to go. Prior administrations had functioned in bureaucratic and antiquated ways, and there was plenty of room for improvement. But that's where I was able to dig in and prove myself.

Besides Sheshunoff, I thankfully had another major source of support in my back pocket: Assistant Controller Dave Martin. With years of experience at WSFS, Dave knew the company inside and out, and was the perfect person to help me get up to speed.

During my first few weeks on the job, Dave pulled out a list of foreclosed properties that the bank owned, and proposed we take a little tour. It was the first time I got to see the tangible examples of where the bank's loans had gone bad. Driving by run-down apartment complexes, vacant townhouses, shuttered restaurants, undeveloped land in bad parts of town, and half-empty strip malls with garbage bags rolling around on the concrete like tumbleweeds, I found myself wondering if I'd made the right career decision. If we'd had another recession at that time, WSFS likely wouldn't have made it.

Doubt resurfaced a few times in my first year at WSFS. I shared my concerns with close friends in the work world. But I also told them about the kind of positive environment I worked in, about my good relationship with Skip, and about the opportunities I saw. They listened and set me straight, telling me that as a person who wanted to make a difference, I was in the right place.

They were right. If I had joined WSFS in hopes of making a mark, it was clear that leaving would be premature. Staying was worth the risk, so I dedicated myself to improving the bank. Soon, another key team member with the same drive for transformation, Karl Johnston, would join me, setting the stage for the next chapter in WSFS' storied history.

TWO | BUILDING BACK A BRAND

By Karl Johnston, as told to Brittany Kriegstein. Karl joined WSFS in 1997 as executive vice president of commercial banking services and became part of a team of irreplaceable players who helped turn the bank's reputation and fortunes around.

One April morning in 1997, around 4 a.m., I was jolted awake by my phone's ring. The caller, an executive at my employer, CoreStates Bank, delivered a piece of news that was both shocking and, in retrospect, foretelling. "Karl, you need to get to the bank. It's on fire."

In an instant, I was out of bed and barreling towards 9th and Market Streets, where the Delaware Trust tower—one of the tallest buildings in Wilmington at the time—loomed over the cityscape. As I arrived, flames were dancing from the upper floors.

The truth is that I had been waiting for a reason to leave my job, and this certainly seemed like one. Coincidentally, WSFS headquarters—much humbler in stature—stood directly across the street.

Looking up at the inferno, I made a pivotal decision: it was time to move on. I was ready for a new challenge, but where to? The banking industry was in the throes of a merger frenzy that was eroding customer service and loyalty. I was eager to find a place where I could forge a better path.

A Résumé Killer

As hard as it is to imagine now, in the early '90s, WSFS was not exactly the jewel of Delaware's banking world, and not an institution that outsiders aspired to join. I'd lived in Delaware since I was a young teen, and had watched the bank slowly lose its prestige in the marketplace, tarnished by years of bad decisions and negative headlines. Yet, this was precisely why I saw an opportunity: to be part of a turnaround at a company grappling with its future.

My gut told me Skip was the right leader for this endeavor; he was a big thinker with integrity and a strategic vision. It was obvious to me that he still had some issues to work out in the bowels of the bank, but as our conversations proceeded, I learned more about his achievements as CEO. The worst appeared to be in the rearview mirror. He was confidence-inspiring, and I believed he would provide me the autonomy to write and execute the commercial banking plan. I had a good reputation in the community, which I was confident I could lean on to boost our business.

In January of 1997, I started as executive vice president of commercial banking services—the last of four new "pillars" Skip had hired to build for the future. I joined a young Mark Turner, who was hired as controller; Tom Stevenson, the chief information officer; and Joe Murphy, head of retail banking.

Building Back a Brand

Starting afresh at any organization comes with its set of hurdles: meeting people, navigating office politics, learning new ways. But at WSFS, my challenge was much greater. It would mean changing how people thought about the business, developing new processes and technology, establishing a completely new credit culture, transitioning people into new roles, upgrading talent, developing new products and services and, last but not least, bringing the bank's reputation back. I would have to demonstrate to the business community—especially my network of prior commercial clients—that WSFS was capable, dependable, and could meet all their financial needs. This was not just about changing tires, it was about changing the entire machine.

On my first day, I swapped the grandiose views and perks of the Delaware Trust tower for a modest office overlooking the State Building. Within the first hour, Skip called me to a meeting in the boardroom with a client who had just defaulted on a large commercial real estate loan. I didn't even get a chance to visit the lunchroom before encountering a major credit problem. That's when the reality hit that this was not going to be easy, especially when progress would be hampered by previous mistakes.

The surprises kept coming. As I worked to assess the abilities of the associates I now managed, I quickly found that many of them lacked the experience, technical knowledge, and customer service skills to oversee loans to larger and more complex businesses. Unlike the kind of lending involved in commercial real estate, which tends to be transactional and price-driven, commercial business lending is built on long-term and trusted relationships. While it can ultimately be very profitable, it means finding and sticking with our clients through their ups and downs—which requires bankers who have both strong sales and risk-assessment competencies. WSFS didn't have enough of that kind of talent.

Rebuilding the bank's reputation was no small feat. Its history as a recently troubled thrift institution meant the brand failed to inspire the best and most profitable clientele. Business owners pick their banks very carefully, and change their banks very rarely.

Shifting perceptions would require big pivots in strategy, but I was confident that we could succeed if we were disciplined, innovative, and realistic about our path forward. The banking climate was ripe for another strong, locally owned financial institution to assert itself in our market, especially as customers grew disenchanted with impersonal service from the sprawling out-of-state banks that swallowed smaller competitors.

Not everyone shared my optimism. One jaded senior manager mocked my ambitions, dismissing me as a delusional dreamer, secretly telling others: *This guy thinks we're going to be the best commercial bank in the state of Delaware. We're never going to be anything but a third-rate commercial real estate lender.*

Meanwhile, an old classmate—now a senior executive at a rival bank—questioned my judgment: *Karl, what are you doing? If you wanted a career change, why didn't you call me? You don't want to have WSFS on your résumé.*

Climbing Out of the Ditch

The skepticism I faced only fueled my determination. Before anything else, WSFS would need a solid road map for its new strategy. So I drafted the credit policy and procedures manual, which was officially adopted as our blueprint for commercial business lending. It would determine what kinds of loans we'd make, to whom, how much risk was acceptable, and more. If everything went well, it would be the foundation for the rebirth of the WSFS brand.

Then I pulled in the right people, reaching out to former CoreStates colleagues with whom I'd had a good rapport, who shared my vision and drive. It wasn't easy. Getting through to solid bankers like Doug Quaintance and Jim Noon meant convincing them to leave promising careers at CoreStates when they had families to support and college tuitions to pay. Despite the risks, they too wanted to be part of something new, to be at the starting line of a competitive race, to make a real impact on shaping the vision of this underdog bank.

To elevate the existing team, I became somewhat of a professor, running loan committee meetings like classes that sometimes lasted four or five hours. We did a lot of analytical training, emphasizing the importance of understanding the concepts of business cycles, working capital, free cash flow, and debt service coverage. It was an exhausting process, and I eventually realized that a very large percentage of the staff still had to be turned over.

To fill those vacancies, I began scouting the halls of WSFS, dropping in unannounced at the offices of younger associates, often several levels down the chain of command. I was looking for people who were bright, hard-working, and eager for an opportunity to be part of something new and different. I emphasized a shift towards relationship-based banking, focusing on client delight to set WSFS apart in an industry increasingly dominated by impersonal mega-banks. To be able to serve a diverse range of businesses and personal wealth needs, WSFS *had* to put the customers first. If we followed that strategy, I was confident that our level of service would exceed expectations.

The next several years would see us take some significant steps in the right direction. Our increasing credibility as an institution would help me convince many members of my old commercial team at CoreStates—mostly former Delaware Trust team members (Delaware Trust merged with Meridian in 1987)—to join WSFS, setting off momentum that encouraged other top talent to seek us out. We'd also reexamine and refresh our brand identity, defining what WSFS really stood for. I'd have exciting opportunities to help design new bank branches that were modern and welcoming, attracting new customers through our dedication to service.

No doubt, I am proud to have played a meaningful part in laying a strong foundation for WSFS, where the cornerstone is based on solid discipline, an unwavering credit culture, professionalism, and a clear set of best practices. But more than anything, I am grateful for the gifted people that joined us along the way, bringing tremendous intellect and enthusiasm to our mission.

The road ahead would test our mettle but, with a clear strategy, a growing culture, and a committed team, I was confident we could transform WSFS into a banking institution that not only survived but thrived.

THREE | THE WORLD'S SMALLEST MONEY CENTER BANK?

By Mark Turner

As Karl diligently reorganized and reinforced the internal framework of our organization, the external landscape was evolving rapidly. The economy was good and industry consolidation was heating up.

From the vantage point of outsiders, WSFS appeared to be on reasonably solid footing. The financial stability that had eluded us during the early 1990s was finally within reach, thanks to Skip and then–vice chair CG Cheleden's heroic efforts. Under their stewardship, we had navigated through the tumultuous waters of near-collapse and emerged with a reclaimed regulatory stature and a solid capital base. Karl, Joe, and Tom were reviving the WSFS infrastructure, workforce, and brand, and we laid a robust foundation for growth. As a team, we set about charting a course for the future, putting together a strategy statement about our intention to be a great community bank—but also allowing for unique investments that enhanced shareholder value. This flexible strategy would let Skip fully explore his entrepreneurial side. But there were also past problems to put to bed.

The Head Injury Property

One of my first challenges involved a particularly intriguing task: the "Head Injury Property." This facility, designed to care for people with severe head trauma, had once seemed a promising undertaking. However, the owners had overbuilt, and found they could not sustain their robust operations with the revenue from patients and the government. They could not repay the loan WSFS had given them, so patients were transferred elsewhere, and foreclosure followed.

By the time I engaged with this asset, it had become a substantial liability, weighing on our asset quality and capital ratios, and drawing severe regulatory criticism. To get rid of a continuing headache, we had to sell. But how?

Recognizing the complexities involved, I took on the role of mediator between WSFS and the distressed property, potential buyers, the accountants, and regulators. The solution we devised was complex yet effective: WSFS would provide a fully secured loan to a local finance company with unique tax attributes to facilitate the property's purchase at its book value. The transaction not only relieved us of a significant liability at no loss, but also freed up capital, added a good loan to our books, and generated ongoing guaranteed income.

This episode was emblematic of the creative strategies needed to navigate our transformation, shedding prior burdens while moving the bank forward.

Ascending to the CFO Role

My successful handling of the Head Injury Property demonstrated to Skip, Bill, and the WSFS leadership that I had both the discipline and ingenuity necessary for the role of CFO of a progressive organization. When Bill announced his retirement in the winter of 1998, a path opened for my promotion.

Bill was a major advocate for me, as were several board members. They knew I was green, but saw that I was a hard worker who was capable of growing quickly into the role; that I was someone who would be continually trying to prove I was worth the risk. Bill had a strong personal philosophy about identifying people who were ripe for advancement, and then mentoring and training them assiduously, as I say "Reaching down, pulling them up, and coaching them up." We have tried to repay him over the years by doing the same for others, like Christine E. Davis, once a senior auditor, now WSFS' executive vice president, chief risk officer; and Shari Kruzinski, once a promising retail banker and now EVP of retail banking.

While Bill, along with others in the organization, were supporters of my promotion into the position of CFO, I was still 35 years old, which was very young for a CFO at a public company. Despite my close relationship with Skip, he couldn't put blinders on and promote me without question, even though I was the only internal candidate. He was obligated to do a thoughtful search.

In interviews and discussions, I worked diligently to convince Skip of my readiness and eventually he came to the same conclusion. In May 1998, I was promoted to the role of CFO. The promotion was both exhilarating and daunting from the weight

of filling Bill's shoes and the immense responsibility of oversee-
ing WSFS' financial health. One of my new duties, for example,
was signing my name onto all the bank's official filings. There are
very few people in an organization who can be tried in criminal
court for misstatements and misdeeds, real or perceived, and the
CFO is at the top of the list.

But I relished the opportunity to make a difference. Now, two
years into my tenure, I realized that WSFS was where I wanted to
be for the rest of my professional career. Despite my readiness to
face these challenges, the pressure was palpable.

The Launching Point

In my new position, I was responsible for dealing with a number of innovative endeavors that extended beyond conventional
banking practices. WSFS and Skip were developing the reputation for taking on more unusual projects. And not long after my
promotion, I worked to further shore up the bank's capital by
issuing trust-preferred securities—a hybrid financing instrument
that looked like debt, but functioned as capital for regulatory
purposes. This elevated WSFS' standing among regulators and
in the market, bolstering us to pursue a growth strategy.

Over the next several years, WSFS explored more than a dozen
interesting investment opportunities, executing them with vary-
ing degrees of success. We embraced a very entrepreneurial spirit,
extending our support to management teams from non-banks
seeking to deliver banking-adjacent products and services through
WSFS. Joe Murphy once famously said, "This management team

has never met a deal it didn't like." That was hyperbole, but made its point. We were a pioneer in what is now known as banking as a service (BaaS). We positioned ourselves as offering the essential bank charter, resources, and oversight that allowed our partners to clear the hurdles of getting into the bank marketplace, and focus on their vision. In doing so, we hoped we would all benefit.

Our bold ventures included subprime credit—a risky but potentially lucrative territory. Subprime lending, with its inherent high credit losses, and reputation and regulatory risks, required vigilant management. We tried to be careful about the kind of subprime lending that we would comfortably take on, eventually choosing to sponsor a credit card for a New York–based furniture rental company. This credit card allowed lower-income customers to furnish their homes, a concept that seemed straightforward but proved more complex in practice. The geographical disconnect between WSFS in Delaware, and the furniture company in New York, created challenges in oversight and monitoring. And, over time, we discovered that the business partner's integrity was questionable, leading to regulatory concerns.

As CFO, it fell upon me to orchestrate a careful exit from this partnership, something far easier said than done. Navigating this process required delicate negotiations with business partners and regulators, and deft planning to mitigate the fallout. I helped us back out of that driveway slowly, and once we were safely out, we notched new experiences and insights about how not to make this kind of mistake again.

Leasing and Losing

During the mid-to-late '90s, we greatly expanded our car leasing business. Although WSFS had been financing car leasing since the early '90s, it was an ancillary business, operating through local dealerships. However, the business expanded under the leadership of a bold executive. He added many new dealerships, then ventured into new territory: West Virginia, far outside our traditional market.

Initially, the expansion seemed promising. But then automakers began subsidizing leases, inflating the projected residual values of vehicles to make lease payments cheaper. This tactic, while effective for moving more cars in the short term, created an unsustainable bubble. As the millennium turned, it became evident that these inflated values were not real. Residual values had plummeted, and the gap between assumed and actual vehicle values widened. We had to absorb those losses. And absorb them we did—WSFS found itself holding the bag on tens of millions of dollars as used vehicle values nosedived, and cars came off lease.

We initially chose to stick with the leasing business, hoping for a turnaround. But reality proved unforgiving. It became clear that car leasing, as it was then structured, was unprofitable and unsustainable for us. My analysis of the situation was the primary impetus behind the decision that this was not a good business for us in the long term if we were always subject to the whims of car manufacturers. While we'd been able to pull off sales of businesses when past endeavors didn't work out, the car leasing company was different: After surveying the market, we quickly realized that we wouldn't be able to sell this distressed business for a rational amount. Instead, we'd have to "discontinue operations"—meaning we'd simply have to manage the business's wind-down ourselves, and eat the future losses.

ATM Services: A Business Started from Inside

In 1996, a law was passed allowing for the charging of a fee for the convenience of customers taking their money out of ATMs. Over the next few years, small companies known as Independent Sales Organizations (ISOs), were popping up all over to put ATMs in hotels, airports, malls, convenience stores, etc. These entrepreneurs were excellent at site selection, but they needed other services, primarily cash, to run the machines. Tom Stevenson, our chief information officer at the time, had come to WSFS with an ATM background. Tom spotted the opportunity to be the bank for these entrepreneurs, and he soon built a new business for WSFS, called Cash Connect, to serve this new industry.

The business had a very rough beginning. Tracking cash across thousands of machines, money vaults, armored car carriers, and electronic switches proved difficult. We also discovered the presence of sticky hands in that chain: money was stolen, usually by insiders. In the late '90s and early 2000s, there were several times when we had to report the missing money as temporary losses, and it would take us months—and huge internal efforts—to find it or recover it through insurance policies. Understandably, we received tremendous pressure from both our board and investors, wondering if this business made sense.

We believed it did and stuck with it. Over time, Tom and his team found ever more trustworthy companies and partners to do business with, and the team implemented solid contracts, tracking, controls, and insurance that would button-down our operations. Over the next 25-plus years, this business incurred no net operational or credit losses, and added many more services that were very profitable. In fact, for most years, it added greatly to the profitability metrics of the bank. So, not all our interesting ventures were achieved with outsiders; Cash Connect was the best example of our "intrapreneurial" spirit.

Everbank: The Digital Gamble

As the world geared up for the start of a new millennium, internet-only banking was taking the industry by storm. While it promised ease for people looking to make quick transactions, it also threatened to disrupt the very kind of people-oriented banking that was the core foundation of the way we did business. Going "from bricks to clicks" in the banking world was the talk of the industry in 1999, but it also wasn't uncommon for bank leaders to ignore or dismiss what seemed like a tidal wave that was fast advancing.

Proactive companies were heading in a variety of different directions. Some banks were responding to the "internet age" by making rudimentary websites, without any content or portals for online banking—just to be able to say that they were already part of the game. They figured those features would come later; unless, of course, the internet didn't stick.

But even that kind of baseline effort could have huge rewards: Sovereign Bank, in Reading, Pennsylvania, was trading at $12 a share until they joined the frenzy by putting up a website. It was little more than a splash page. But almost overnight, their valuation doubled to $24.

Pressure loomed at WSFS. One prominent investor called Skip, insisting, *You gotta do this, just announce that you're doing something.* But we wanted to take a more substantive approach.

After some discussion, we partnered with an entrepreneur who had already done a lot of work in establishing a real internet bank—not just a website for display. He already had the plumbing, so to speak: a team, a product set, and the know-how to make this whole online dream into a productive reality.

Our partner's concept, Everbank, was innovative, and went beyond domestic banking, offering non-dollar-denominated deposits—essentially foreign currency accounts housed in an American-based bank with FDIC insurance. This was not just about having an internet presence; it was about having a competitive edge. Our investment of approximately $5 million bought us a 25 percent stake.

It was an exciting prospect, positioning us at the forefront of digital banking with a unique twist. However, things soon unraveled. Our initial plan to structure their deposits and loans off WSFS' balance sheet was thwarted by regulators who demanded more oversight and integration with our financial records. WSFS found itself fully entangled in Everbank's operations and start-up losses.

The complications were many. Instead of being a relatively passive investor, WSFS was now a functional full owner, and the losses started to mount. After a challenging three years, we managed to sell it to a Florida-based mortgage company at book value. While we avoided further losses, the experience was costly in terms of both time and effort. It was certainly a hiccup for our new experimental strategy, and an additional headache for those of us on the leadership team. For me—the new and perfectionist CFO who was anxious about the possibility of failure—it was especially brutal.

These losses notwithstanding, engaging in joint ventures with entrepreneurial management teams was advantageous for us. In some cases, we benefited significantly from our ownership share. But even if they proved financially unsuccessful, we learned new and best practices and technologies, which would impact our thinking for years to come. And, as we did more of these projects, we learned how to do them better. Everbank was costly, but we learned how to support entrepreneurs to be pioneers, while at the same time protecting our bank's balance sheet, income statement, and reputation. This was a hard line to walk, but we made it work by setting up key guardrails, things like requiring a separate charter for the joint venture after a short start-up time; requesting monthly fees and transaction fees for the services we provided; and requiring ultimate control of quality assurance functions like audit, compliance, and new product launches. These were "musts" that we implemented for similar ventures going forward.

United Asian Bank

Amidst the whirlwind of new projects, WSFS embarked on another ambitious venture catering to the local Korean American community. The idea stemmed from an influential Korean American professor who our then-COO Karl Johnston had studied with at the University of Delaware, who was very involved in that bustling community outside of Philadelphia. He persuaded WSFS to establish United Asian Bank in Cheltenham, Pennsylvania, targeting this underserved and vibrant demographic.

The premise was sound: a bank that understood and spoke the language of its community. Sure, these account holders could go to the banks that already existed in the area, but it was clear that the community would be much more trusting of a company that understood their culture. It was a familiar story in WSFS history: CG Cheleden, a particularly influential prior WSFS board investor, then–chair and eventual lead director who we'll hear from later, grew up working at the Lithuanian bank his parents had started almost 100 years earlier.

However, the reality proved far more complex. From translating all the bank materials into Korean to tailoring every aspect of products, operations, and technology to fit the Korean lifestyle, the project became a massive undertaking. The logistical and cultural hurdles quickly became apparent. It didn't make sense for WSFS to devote so many unique resources to a relatively small effort, and we already had our hands in so many different pots.

Despite our best efforts, it was clear that running a small Korean bank within an American bank was beyond our capacity. By 2002, we decided to sell United Asian Bank to nearby National

Penn Bank. Although we made a modest gain, the endeavor highlighted our limitations in managing small, highly specialized ventures. Nevertheless, some of the Korean American associates who were part of the project continued their careers with WSFS, serving the Asian American community around Washington, DC, in a more manageable fashion, and adding a lasting diversity to our operations.

Branching Out

By this point, WSFS was growing sturdier, and we were seeking ways to reach outward beyond our home turf in Wilmington and northern Delaware. What better way to do that than to focus on new branches?

In 1999, WSFS was already well-established with a family-owned supermarket chain named Genuardi's, whose roots stretched back to the 1920s. Since its start, Genuardi's had grown from a humble produce wagon into a prominent supermarket brand in the greater Philadelphia area. Their stores were renowned for their quality, and their community feel, making them an ideal partner for WSFS. We dipped our toes into that pool by putting a few branches within Genuardi's stores.

Supermarket banking turned out to be convenient for Genuardi's customers—and happy customers made Genuardi's want to build up their partnership with us. They proposed adding a bank branch to 15 or 20 of their stores in Pennsylvania and Delaware, and it seemed like a perfect, low-cost way to expand our franchise. With fifteen to twenty thousand people passing by the

WSFS logo in each store on a weekly basis, we figured new customers would fall easily into place.

We were wrong. The first dozen WSFS branches that rolled out in Genuardi's in Pennsylvania ended up being little more than very expensive ATMs. We soon realized that we had to do all new marketing: not only for customers, but for potential associates who didn't recognize the WSFS name. While in-store banking was convenient for our existing customers within our footprint, it did not translate well to attracting new customers because potential new customers had long-standing relationships with other banks, and were reluctant to switch in the supermarket setting. In the end, the branches, customers, and deposits were sold to PNC at our book value, meaning there was no gain for us.

Still, this venture provided valuable insights. We learned that in-store branches were effective only within a familiar footprint, and that attracting new customers required more than just strategic placement. Despite the challenges, we were among the pioneers of large-scale in-store banking, bolstering our reputation for innovation.

Reverse Mortgages

Back in 1988—well before we became involved with supermarket branches, subprime credit, and all the other non-traditional endeavors we eventually pursued—the bank loaned $10 million to American Homestead, a reverse mortgage company doing business in New Jersey. Reverse mortgages were generally taken out by people over 60 who had substantial home equity and needed to increase their monthly cash flow to live comfortably. A lender would appraise the property to determine its value, and then make a prediction on the homeowner's life expectancy. They'd try to pin down just how much the home's value might increase during those golden years. Then, that information would be used to determine how much cash the lender could send to the homeowner, usually in the form of a monthly check. If the calculation was correct, and the homeowner lived for as long as projected, there would be sufficient equity for the home to be sold and the loan terms to be paid off in full. If the calculation was faulty, the lender could lose a lot of money. American Homestead lost a lot of money, could not repay our loan, and we got a large slice of their reverse mortgages as collateral for that loan gone bad.

Skip didn't find out about the bank's investment until just before he joined the company, when he sat with accountants from Price Waterhouse to do his full review of the bank's dealings. It was clear that American Homestead's loan formula was deeply flawed, and even the assets we picked up were impaired.

But those weren't the only reverse mortgages WSFS had by the time I joined the bank. In 1994, having gained some hard-earned knowledge about reverse mortgage valuations, Skip bought another portfolio of reverse mortgages from a struggling San Francisco–based company called Providential Home Income Plan, the first company to go public whose sole business line was reverse mortgages. When California real estate ran into trouble in the early '90s, Providential also ran into trouble—and it was a good opportunity for WSFS to step in. Few other bankers comprehended how reverse mortgages worked, so no one else was interested in trying to make a deal.

WSFS emerged from the acquisition with one of the largest private sector reverse mortgage portfolios in the country, and these were at a great price.

The real estate market did not tank. Rather, it exploded—especially in California. By 2002, we were approached by executives from Lehman Brothers who wanted to establish a market in the securitization of reverse mortgages: a process by which certain types of assets are pooled so that they can be repackaged and offered in slices based on the differing risk levels investors want. Our reverse mortgages, seasoned and stable, were ripe for this process.

Paul Greenplate, our treasurer; and Rom Gac, a key member of our treasury team, played crucial roles in managing the complex sale. The ultimate outcome was spectacular—$175 million from portfolios that originally cost us $20 to $30 million.

This was a misunderstood, extremely undervalued asset. Not only did we recognize that, and purchase Providential at a great price, but we stuck with it—through thick and thin, including PR pressure, investor misunderstanding, funky accounting and tax attributes, and the ups and downs of real estate values that sometimes swung our income wildly. If there's any episode that really defines our spirit, culture, and stick-to-it-ness, it's our history with reverse mortgages.

The capital it generated was transformative for WSFS. "The big moment was really that securitization," Paul remembers now. "By taking that capital, we were able to grow the bank in other ways—the acquisitions we made in the 2010s, and all the little banks we started purchasing. We wouldn't have been able to do that without the sale and securitization of those reverse mortgages."

An epilogue: In 2003, we were sued by the original owners of American Homestead. They claimed that, according to our contract, we owed them more money for their small slice of the sale than we paid them. We were adamant that we paid them very fairly. I took the lead in our defense, which entailed many weeks of research and calculations; working with lawyers and experts; drafting briefs and defense strategies; sitting for depositions; and being our primary defense coordinator and lead witness. The stress manifested as back pain that had me doubled over at times, but we won the case—on all counts. This was important because it saved us millions of dollars, and protected our reputation in the market as being a fair dealer, which we would need as we pursued other partnerships and acquisitions in years to come.

Near-Prime Mortgages, Super-Prime Results

Our foray into subprime finance wasn't just a series of experiments; it was a strategic exploration of new opportunities. Enter JC Faulkner, a successful subprime mortgage entrepreneur based in Charlotte, North Carolina, who was looking to find a partner for his business in 1999. While his business was ultimately deemed too big for us, our relationship with JC paid off when he introduced us to Jerry Schiano, a former executive at a non-prime mortgage company, who was setting up a new venture in the subprime space after the big company he worked for went out of business. Jerry knew the perils of the subprime mortgage world, and his vision was to "build a better mousetrap" in the industry, which was then experiencing significant upheaval.

The proposal was straightforward: WSFS would provide $3 million in start-up funds and other resources, including a charter, and Jerry's company would generate mortgages in our name—selling them quickly to third parties, focusing on what he termed "near-prime" mortgages.

That proposal resonated with us. In 1999, we met with him and his new team many times to try to find out as much as possible about what we'd be getting ourselves into.

The initial year was fraught with challenges. The new venture faced logistical issues, and building a market presence from scratch proved difficult. Jerry's company burned through our cash faster than anticipated, but the relationship remained promising. In the chapter to follow, Jerry tells the story of our venture's rough start—and its stunning success.

Too Big or Too Small?

By early 2002, we had built a collection of far-flung, interesting, ambitious businesses inside the bank, and people noticed. We weren't exactly behaving like a community bank, nor could we successfully aim for the ranks of international money center banks like JP Morgan, Bank of America, or Barclays. One Boston investor wryly commented, when Skip and I met him on a road show, "I call you guys 'the world's smallest money center bank.'" It was a strategic tension that we would need to deal with in the very near future.

FOUR | A TRUE PARTNER

By Jerry Schiano, as told to Brittany Kriegstein. Jerry is an enterprising visionary who forged three strategic partnerships with WSFS in collaborations that, over time, yielded remarkable financial returns.

From the start, I was impressed by Skip and Mark. WSFS, known for its prudent banking practices and strategic gambles, saw promise in my background, and I felt an immediate rapport with them. We all wanted to ensure we got everything right.

After a series of strategy meetings, WSFS decided against acquiring an existing mortgage entity. Instead we opted to build one from scratch, together. This was no hasty decision; setting up the structure required meticulous planning. Despite my previous experience in the industry, this was my first foray into launching a company from the ground up. We were all keenly aware of the stakes, and determined to navigate every detail with precision. In 1999, amidst much hope and excitement, Wilmington National Finance was born.

I had no idea that four or five months later I'd be grappling with an unpleasant reality check (it was flailing). I thought I knew exactly what we needed to do to create a successful lending business, but it wasn't working. Our competitors had already established relationships with brokers and loan buyers and, as a result, were much more comfortable making loan decisions, and had better service. And I still had some scars from the company I'd previously worked for, where credit quality issues abounded. Determined not to make those poor lending mistakes, I was too timid, and it affected my leadership and my team. In short, I learned the hard way that planning a business and starting a business are two very different things.

I went to Skip and Mark and said, "Guys, this isn't what I thought would happen. And we're going to pull back until we figure it out."

Looking back, it was the best decision I could have made. Skip and Mark didn't just nod sympathetically—they actively stepped up. I clearly remember Mark saying, "What can we do to help you be successful?" We crafted a loan that WSFS would purchase to get the operations flowing and instill confidence in our staff. This gesture provided the exact lift we needed, setting us on a path to market acceptance, growth, and profitability. Ironically, despite their crucial support, we didn't end up selling many loans to WSFS over the years. What mattered was that they gave us the credibility and confidence to move forward, and that was invaluable.

In the often-tumultuous world of entrepreneurship, relationships with partners can be fraught with tension. They invest time, money, and resources, and if the venture falters, everyone feels the sting. But rather than abandoning ship, Skip and Mark chose to stand by us. They could have been disillusioned or confrontational, but they instead became true partners. They appreciated my deliberate approach to quality and spending, and I deeply valued their willingness to support me through thick and thin.

We would go on to partner in three profitable ventures.

True leadership is demonstrated not when everything is going smoothly, but when things go awry. Eventually, we not only met our goals at Wilmington National Finance, but we exceeded them astronomically, and were approached by a buyer who presented us with, as they say, a good problem to have.

Without a doubt, the WSFS leaders I've gotten to work with are extraordinary. They focus on risk and compliance, but they also make interesting investments. And, as an outsider looking in, a lot of them are very successful.

Mark would always be the one who asked the tough questions. None of them were ever pushovers by any means, but Mark especially so. He's firm—you gotta know your stuff. No B.S. Any business has strengths and weaknesses, but any weakness we had, we could always count on Mark Turner to ask us about. He's very analytical and very perceptive, and he will ask the challenging questions that will ultimately make you rise to the occasion.

Sometimes people who are good number twos can't become good number ones because it's a different skill set. But when Mark stepped into the CEO role, I saw his relationship and strategic sides, in addition to his analytical side.

I'm not a huge fan of big banks, but there can be downsides to smaller banks too. The thing that sets WSFS apart is this personality that has been created by Skip, Mark, and now Rodger. You couldn't ask for more in a set of leaders, partners, or bankers.

When I started with WSFS, they were a little bank that was just coming out of trouble. And now they've become one of the premier banking institutions in the Delaware and Philadelphia area. It's amazing to see.

FIVE | HIGH HIGHS
AND LOW LOWS

By Mark Turner

I n business, there are moments when everything just clicks—
when the stars align and success is palpable. That was us in
late 2002, only three years after we launched Jerry's company. The economy was humming, and Jerry possessed acute
skills as a leader, operator, and deal maker.

The company grew so quickly that it began to outpace our
ability to support it with capital. Jerry's expanding network of
business relationships meant we were no longer essential to his
growth. It was a bittersweet realization.

Then came the grand offer. American General Finance, a
subsidiary of American International Group (AIG), wanted to
buy Jerry's company for over $120 million. With WSFS holding
an 80 percent stake, we pocketed an impressive $100 million.
Our steadfast commitment had paid off spectacularly. It was a
remarkable return on our original $3 million investment, just
three years earlier.

To put our success in perspective, consider this: In the final
quarter of 2002, we sold our reverse mortgages; and on the very
first day of 2003, Jerry's company changed hands. In just a few

months we racked up over $200 million in gains, doubling our capital base. It had taken WSFS 170 years to build the capital we already had, and we more than doubled it in one quarter.

This massive win was the result of management making good risk/reward decisions, a disciplined approach to entering and exiting markets at the right times, finding good partners, executing with excellence, and staying the course through periods of turbulence.

Still, I'd be remiss if I didn't acknowledge that companies like Lehman Brothers and AIG chasing riskier assets at the wrong times during that period eventually revealed deeper systemic issues that would come to a head in 2008. Had WSFS retained those assets heading into the financial crisis, the market's heightened skepticism, the subsequent collapse in asset values, and the actual and projected impact on our capital could have resulted in a run on the bank—resulting in our failure. We were able to maximize gains and get out of dangerous territory just before the big problems hit, thanks to disciplined leadership and good risk management.

Breakdown

The very projects that had fueled those one-time gains created some turbulence within the bank. Our many ventures had increasingly distracted us from our core market, and the question on everyone's mind was, "Are we still a community bank?" This confusion bred cultural rifts, and left many investors puzzled.

The many new projects we plunged into were far ranging

and outside of conventional community banking. Skip, the architect of these ventures, relied on me to bring his visions to life, and keep them on track. I was the one navigating the intricate web of partnerships, vendors, accountants, lawyers, regulators, and investors.

And when things got messy, I cleaned them up. The workload was staggering, and the stress was unrelenting. The scrutiny from regulators, investors, and associates was constant. Juggling these responsibilities took a toll on me physically and emotionally. I learned a ton, but also aged a ton.

Adding to the mix, at that time, was my decision to pursue a full-time executive MBA at Wharton; and start a family with my wife, Regina. My life was a juggling act of things risky, exciting, and new—WSFS, school, and family responsibilities—leaving me stretched to the breaking point.

By late 2002, my body finally staged a revolt. I wasn't taking care of myself, and I came down with the worst possible version of the flu—I couldn't keep anything in, not even water. It got so bad that I took myself to the emergency room because my muscles were seizing up. They put me on an intravenous drip, and got some water back in my body, but it wasn't a long-term fix. Two days later, I felt even worse, and Regina had to drive me back to the ER. I was hospitalized for almost three days with extreme dehydration, but I must have blacked out because I don't remember much of my stay at all.

When I was discharged from the hospital and returned to work, Linda Drake, one of the board members, asked me what happened. After I explained, she looked at me with such kindness and said something to the effect of, *Please, don't ever let that happen again.* She was right: I was working so hard that I'd let the most important thing—my health—fall apart. Not many people knew this then, but I'd had my colon removed in my early 30s due to a severe case of ulcerative colitis, which had deteriorated into precancerous lesions. Since my digestive tract is compromised, I have to pay more attention to it than most people do. Instead, I had let my body down. The doctors in the hospital told me that if I'd waited much longer, they weren't sure what the outcome would have been.

Emotionally, I was also struggling. I've probably come close to two nervous breakdowns in my life, and this was one of those times because of the sheer level of work and stress. The biggest obstacle of all was the fact that WSFS as a company was strategically confused—wrapped up in nearly a dozen projects that had created a sense of discord with people on the inside, and on the outside. I was the one who had to figure it all out, and explain what was going on, but that was becoming harder and harder to do.

I sought advice from Skip. "I'm the CFO," I said, "and I can't make sense of what we are doing. How am I supposed to explain it to anyone else?"

Skip, ever the calm presence, responded with a question: "What do you do to relieve stress?"

"I run," I said.

"Are you doing that now?"

I answered truthfully, "I don't have the time."

"I don't want you to come to work in the morning until you've gone for a run," he said. "Even if that's 10 o'clock in the morning."

Running, again, became a vital part of my stress relief, strength, and solace, but it wasn't a cure for the underlying issues at the bank. Yet Skip's support was instrumental in helping me navigate this rough patch. When I got to the lowest of lows, Skip stood by me, and was a big part of the reason I was able to stick with the job. When I broke down one day, he sat down next to me, put his arm around me and said, "We're going to get through this."

With the passing years, I've spent plenty of time reflecting on this dark period in my career. I was raised to believe that determination and out-working everyone was the key to being successful—or at least, it was the key to avoiding my absolute worst fear: failure. And hard work *is* important. But it took a collapse to teach me that success and achievement mean nothing without health and wellness, and that health and wellness depend on being humble and human with your circle of colleagues, loved ones, and doctors. If you're struggling, say it. Don't be afraid to ask for help.

I wish I could say I learned this lesson once and for all—but the truth is more complicated. I forget sometimes, and my body reminds me, but I do pay attention better and earlier now.

SIX | A NEW STRATEGY, A NEW TEAM, A NEW CEO

By Mark Turner

Slowly but surely, with support from Skip, the rest of the team, and my running shoes, I was able to weather the stress of the bank's eclectic, experimental period. I emerged stronger and so did WSFS: We had a better idea of our limits, and we were ready to implement a more intentional and focused strategy.

It became clear that we should part ways with some of the projects that had taken up so much time, energy, and concentration. I used the dealmaking skills I had honed over the previous decade to orchestrate a flurry of sales and reductions that would help the bank clean house. Those efforts culminated in just a few months—late 2002 through early 2003—when we sold or wound down a whopping *six* of our previous endeavors. Nothing was a straight line: In all those deals there were twists and turns, highlights, and lowlights that I had to deal with; all while still helping run a public company community bank. I worked my butt off.

Not everyone was thrilled with our new direction. Selling off profitable ventures like the near-prime mortgage business raised eyebrows. Investors worried about lost earnings, and some even dumped their WSFS stock. While the surge in capital from the sales was a huge plus for the bank on paper, it created some uncertainty among company outsiders who worried what WSFS would do with it all. There is a fear, not unfounded, that if you have a lot of capital, you're going to do something stupid with it. To counter this skepticism, we implemented a bold and disciplined stock buy-back program to demonstrate our confidence in our future. As the supply of available shares dwindled, the value of those held by loyal investors increased.

With all of that behind us, now what? It was time to look at WSFS anew, and to determine what the company's way forward should look like.

Building Our Strategy

We embarked on a path of making significant investments in our core franchise: from bringing on new talent in areas like marketing to updating and reimagining existing branches, expanding the branch franchise, building out the commercial business unit, and making more and larger loans. All these actions directly benefited the bank, its associates, and the wider community.

This ensued from a full review of our strategic direction. About a year before the major sales, we began to reimagine WSFS. We brought in an outside consultant to conduct a SWOT analysis—identifying strengths, weaknesses, opportunities, and threats. The conclusion was clear: WSFS' deep community roots were our greatest intangible asset, but we needed to build on that foundation by prioritizing what was most missing in the market, and what we could best deliver— stellar banking service.

Skip's vision was ambitious: We aimed to be "America's best bank for service." It wasn't a catchy slogan, but it became our battle cry. We committed to transforming WSFS into a bank that didn't just talk the talk but walked the walk.

With more experienced staff, better infrastructure, and wider recognition throughout the community, customers and prospective associates alike were starting to think more seriously about WSFS. High-profile commercial clients started giving us a chance too, and recruiting talent became easier. We were no longer seen as a second or third choice, but as a formidable player in the market. We were rebuilding our reputation.

Karl's efforts were instrumental. A few years earlier, he'd been offered a CEO position somewhere else—and felt ready to move on. But Skip knew how important Karl was to our development, so we struck a deal: Karl and I would both be elevated into the "office of the CEO," joining Skip in a partnership of sorts where we'd both take on additional responsibilities. It was a genius construct by Skip, keeping both Karl and I in the fold, and motivating us even more. Along with his work on the commercial side of the company, Karl would now also run the retail side—our revenue-generating divisions in the front of house, so to speak. I was put in charge of all the support divisions, like finance, audit, HR, and technology.

With that arrangement in place, Karl dove even further into our vision for the future. He brought in key players from his old commercial team at CoreStates—mostly former Delaware Trust associates—to join WSFS. This included key hires like Glenn Kocher for chief credit officer, and Scott Baylis for senior relationship manager, as well as the much-needed members of his previous administrative staff who would handle the day-to-day service requirements of WSFS' new clients.

This new group of experienced loan officers and administrators were not enticed to work at WSFS for job security, or for above-market compensation, as we had a relatively small budget. No, they came because WSFS was investing in a credit and service culture that they personally valued as important to themselves, as well as their customers. And, as we pulled in more capable relationship managers, like Steve Clark—who was viewed as perhaps the best commercial banker in the market—others grew increasingly confident that working for WSFS would be a great move. This larger, hyper-engaged team would set into motion a host of new and enhanced commercial banking products: inventory and equipment financing, business lines of credit, commercial construction financing, small business lending services, SBA financing, private banking services, and treasury and cash management services.

"We Stand For Service" is Born

To cement our initiatives, the bank had to take a fresh look at its advertising. Who were the people involved with the bank? What did "WSFS" stand for, now? Redefining a big company requires the consensus of many, but often the genius of one or two crucial players is best. In this case, we knew we'd have to hire a talented quarterback—someone with the energy, vision, and expertise to drive the new strategy, and take it far into the future.

That person turned out to be Joan Sullivan, a vibrant, creative professional from our vaunted competitor down the street, Wilmington Trust. Aside from building up a new marketing team, one of her first orders of business was hiring a firm called Aloysius Butler & Clark (AB&C) to work on the bank's rebranding.

One of Joan's early insights was that we couldn't just go out and say we were the "best bank for service." People outside *and* inside the organization needed to feel it first—otherwise it would be a hollow claim, and we would lose credibility. She understood the profound truth that your brand is who you really are, and what you really do. So, we focused on improving our culture and service before we rolled out any new branding.

At one point, we also discussed changing the name of the bank. Some members of the leadership team and executive staff thought that having "Wilmington" and "Savings Fund Society" featured so prominently might limit our future geographical expansion beyond Delaware. At the time, I was in the camp that saw those terms as an advantage, not a limitation. Delaware and Wilmington are our roots—a small state and a small city with a small-town feel. Keeping "Wilmington" in our name would help us continually emphasize our commitment to community banking, no matter how or where we expanded. This was a crucial part of our identity that set us apart from other, larger institutions at the time: decision-making would always take place, first and foremost, at our Wilmington headquarters. For advertising, we'd mostly be using our initials anyway.

After a few years of intense work—once we had real data showing that both our associates and customers *believed* we were dedicated to service—we launched AB&C's most lasting contribution: the now-famous "**We Stand For Service**" tagline. The smart, catchy phrase renewed what WSFS stood for, and we felt it embodied everything that WSFS was, and aimed to be. Now, we had to figure out a clever way to bring those words into the hearts and minds of prospective customers. At that time, other banks were simply advertising with their logos—a jumble of letters on a billboard. Karl thought WSFS could do something different, so he came up with an idea for an ad featuring portraits of our bank associates. It would read: "We will meet you over lunch, not over an 800 number." Our associates, who had once shied away from public visibility, now proudly represented WSFS.

The "Service Paradox"

One of our early service tests came in May 2003, when a system update caused customers to see inaccurate balances on their ATM receipts, leading to incorrect overdraft fees. We began to hear rumblings through the grapevine that a few customers were confused and complaining. A couple of weeks later, I got a call from Jonathan Epstein, a local *Wilmington News Journal* reporter, who said a source had told him that they were getting hit with charges when they shouldn't have been.

I remember saying, "Well there's just no way that could happen." He agreed not to do a story right then. But later, on a quiet Saturday, my home phone rang. It was Jonathan, and it was urgent. He said, "Mark, I'm doing a story. I've heard from more people, credible people, that this is happening."

I said, "Jonathan, give me till the end of the day Monday, and I'll get back to you. We will investigate fully. You'll get the whole truth, and I'm not going to try to dissuade you from writing the story."

I probably sounded calm, but I was nervous. We all know how quickly bad press can cause havoc at a bank—even one with a good reputation.

The next few days of trying to get to the bottom of the situation was like a fire drill, because many people in the organization were not aware it was happening, and/or they didn't understand how it could happen in the first place. The following Monday, I had taken the train to Washington, DC for an important conference. I couldn't find a private place to settle in, so at about 8 a.m., I sat down on the floor in a calm corner of Union Station to try to figure out what was going on.

There, among the tall pillars, I hopped on a call with the investigative team to find out what they'd uncovered. They relayed that yes, a mistake had been made; and yes, it was in the system's coding. They had numbers, too: how many people were impacted, how many charges would have to be returned.

I had promised Jonathan that I'd get back to him by Monday, so I had to quickly come up with a solid plan for moving forward. I told Jonathan that he was right, that our customers had been right, and that we were wrong. I detailed what the mistake was, how it happened, and what we were doing to make it right. "We'll fix the problem, identify who was impacted, refund any erroneous fees—and we're going to issue a blanket apology, and apologize to them individually as they call."

As a result, Jonathan's headline ran as "WSFS will Refund Inappropriately Charged Fees." And he used a quote from me that came to define the bank's integrity. *"We don't like to make mistakes, but we believe this affected a small number of our customers for only a short period of time," said Chief Operating Officer Mark Turner. "When we do make mistakes, we do right by our customers, and we're in the process of doing that."*

It ended up being a defining moment in solidifying my leadership, our company, and this new value system we were trying to implement: We do the right thing, we're transparent, we own up to mistakes, we correct problems, we say we're sorry; and we go above and beyond to provide great service, and help people feel good about the organization.

The Service Recovery Paradox is the idea that a skillful service recovery can wind up being more impactful than flawless service in the first place—and it became part of our WSFS ethos.

Building New Branches

On the retail side, in Karl and Joan's vision, WSFS' branches needed to be refreshed and revamped into spaces that would allow the bank's elevated service to shine. New branches were also introduced—and reintroduced—into downstate markets. This created a unique set of challenges, as some of those markets were either unfamiliar with the WSFS name, or were skeptical of a bank that had effectively disappeared from the region

15 years earlier. How could people trust that WSFS was back, and back to stay?

Karl and Joan insisted that the new retail banking offices look unique and welcoming from all sides, but it was hard to find an architect to get that done right. So Karl took out his pencils and sketched the plans himself. After all, the branches were basically additional big billboards for WSFS. They had to be places that people would enjoy going to, they had to display the bank's signature green color, they had to have lots of glass on the exterior, and they couldn't be hidden in the depths of rundown strip malls. The design projected a place that was almost like a café, a place that said "come and visit."

In addition to spearheading that effort, Karl led the charge to add necessary commercial infrastructure—such as merchant services, payment processing services, trade finance products, and more—with help from Jim Noon, Doug Quaintance, and Cathy McCloskey previously from Delaware Trust. With branches that inspired customers to engage with the company, and services that met all their needs, we felt confident that we'd be able to prove our commitment to the marketplace. We weren't that clunky bank anymore that almost failed.

With her intuitive nature, endless enthusiasm, and infectious positivity, Joan breathed life into our cultural blueprint. Tragically, she died of cancer in 2006, shortly after the first branch prototype was built. Every time a customer or associate in one of the cheerful spaces she helped to create says, *I like being here,* it's a testament to her talent and dedication.

Exploring and Expanding
Our Wealth Management Division

In this era, we were also exploring ways to enter the wealth management business, an idea Skip had in the early 2000s. As banks like PNC and others competed for customers and made mistakes, pivotal openings emerged to grasp clients who weren't satisfied. Aside from helping round out the bank's service offerings, the wealth sector would help WSFS to diversify its revenue and earnings streams because it tends to have different cycles than the traditional banking business.

Still, we had to be able to say, resolutely, "We provide these services, and in a better way." To find out how to do that, Skip embarked on a study, which revealed the myriad ways the venture would be challenging. First, the wealth management business has more "sticky" customers than other types of banking—meaning that they choose their providers carefully, and don't switch easily. Half the companies that get into the business fail and get out, and the other half take about 10 years to get to even minimal profitability. To distinguish ourselves as a profitable player in the sector, we'd have to make some deft choices.

We hired a man named Chief (Charles) Burton, who specialized in wealth company acquisitions, to lead the charge. In 2004, his first big move was to strike a deal for WSFS to acquire Cypress Capital Management, a company that managed half a billion dollars in assets from local people and institutions. Started by Dick Arvedlund, a sharp mind in the world of finance and investing, Cypress had a solid regional reputation, and would help us establish a major foothold in the sector in a way that would come to fuller fruition in 2010.

Laying the Groundwork for Future Leadership

As we forged ahead, I began to prepare for the possibility of stepping into the CEO role.

In a meeting in 2002 with Skip that I'll never forget, he said to me, "We love what you're doing, we want you to be here for a long time. What are your plans?"

I told him I wanted to be CEO somewhere, sometime, and that I'd love it if that place could be WSFS. He said, "Great, what's your time frame?" And I remember saying, "In three years I think I'll be ready and green. In seven years I think I'll be ready and antsy. And in five years I think I'll be good and ready." He smiled and replied, "We can work with that."

Still working alongside me in the "Office of the CEO," Karl was also potentially on track for that position. Then life threw him a curveball. Karl was diagnosed with aggressive, stage four prostate cancer. His doctors at Johns Hopkins estimated his chances of survival at only 8 percent, with surgery having a low probability of success—and the added possibility that it could shorten his life even further. It was a heart-wrenching blow.

Karl had spent years solidifying the commercial services division in terms of credit culture, portfolio monitoring and risk management, business development, sales support, systems upgrades, and personnel. In about a decade, he had grown commercial business loans—excluding investment real estate and mortgage loans—from less than $20 million to a stunning $1.3 billion, and grew commercial deposits from $755 million to $1.3 billion.

Despite his grim medical prognosis, Karl pushed on with professionalism and strength—thanks in large part to companionship and motivation from none other than Joan Sullivan, who happened to be fighting her own war with breast cancer at the time.

Not aspiring to become CEO, Karl instead threw his efforts into grooming me for the position. He acted as a mentor, and counselor, and advocated for my development. As time went on, he passed some of his duties on to me, helping me to be better equipped for the role. Karl was incredibly gracious and generous in helping me get to that next level. His mindset was selfless.

At this stage, Skip and the board—especially a few key members and supporters like Dave Hollowell, and former Delaware Governor Dale Wolf—really began to view me as the bank's heir apparent to the top position. The transition of authority and responsibility happened earlier than the official announcement date, a healthy practice in any organization. But it still didn't happen quickly; there were hurdles to clear and hoops to jump through.

Team WSFS Gains More Key Players

I think of the CFO of a company as the chief disciplinarian, and the COO as the one in charge of making the organization move forward. By about 2003, it had become evident that I just couldn't wear both of those hats.

As part of my new set of responsibilities, Skip granted me the green light to bring in more team members, so I worked on finding someone to take one of those roles off my plate. I was also conscious of the fact that whoever I hired to fill our important open positions would be instrumental in shaping WSFS' trajectory for years to come.

First, I hired Steve Fowle, from another bank in the Midwest, to take on the CFO role. He turned out to be a perfect cultural fit for WSFS, and struck a key balance of collegiality and discipline during an important growth phase for our company. Steve stuck with us for more than a decade before leaving for a new opportunity (and sunnier weather) in Florida.

Second, retail banking needed a transformative leader, and Rick Wright, who joined us around 2004, was our answer. Rick revolutionized our retail approach with the Universal Associate Model. His strategy was simple yet radical: Any associate at any branch should be able to handle any task. Instead of "Sorry, that person isn't here right now, come back later," it became "I can help you with that." This service-oriented mindset made WSFS a trailblazer in the banking industry. As I've often said, Rick took us from being a third-rate retail banking organization to the best in the market.

We also hired on other key positions, like a new Chief Information Officer Barbara Fischer, who, along with her successor, Jim Mazarakis, were team players, and deeply understood technology's role in business and banking.

Critically, with Karl nearing retirement at this point, the search for a new head of commercial lending was on. This was no small task—commercial lending was becoming the crown jewel of WSFS, and finding Karl's successor was crucial.

After a few months, with the help of Alan Kaplan from the recruiting firm Kaplan Partners, a front-runner named Rodger Levenson emerged. A Philly-area native like me, with a stellar track record at CoreStates and Citizens Bank, Rodger seemed to embody everything WSFS needed. I felt an immediate connection with him—he was the kind of guy who would both stretch our team, and mesh easily with them.

The final hurdle was convincing Rodger that WSFS was the right fit for him. I showed him the nearly completed new building, and pointed out his future office. It was less about the bricks and mortar and more about signaling that WSFS was on the ascent. We were making strides, investing in our future, and achieving high visibility. This last pitch was vital to tipping the scales in our favor.

Rodger joined us in late 2006, and his tenure was nothing short of transformative. His skills and experience dispelled any early awkwardness about his appointment over internal candidates. Together, we made a lot of promotions and hires, guided by the principle that we'd prefer to have a team of eights and nines out of 10—that operate at an 11—rather than a lot of 10s who only operate together at a six or seven because they tend to be self-absorbed and hyper-competitive. We were focused on the best team we could build.

To be perfectly honest, not every hire worked out. Some had come from much bigger banks, and weren't prepared for the kinds of responsibilities and initiatives they'd be expected to take on at WSFS; others didn't share the same focus on openness, honesty, and transparency. What we ultimately learned is that people who didn't align with our values and culture might be good people, but weren't good fits for the company—and that wasn't healthy for them or us.

Still, we didn't want uniformity; we wanted diversity within our value system. We needed people who could stretch us, and not merely conform to a predetermined "Stepford Associate" mold. It became clear that distinguishing between value differences and style differences was essential. People could have varied styles while sharing the same core values, and that was something to be encouraged.

Stepping Up to the Plate

After five years of careful grooming by Skip, the board, and Karl, I was finally nearing the finish line to become CEO. Skip had made it abundantly clear through his actions that I was next in line, so my promotion wasn't a shock to anyone. Still, it was a momentous occasion.

The transition was set to coincide with the bank's April 2007 annual meeting, a colossal undertaking in and of itself. I was juggling the earnings release, the board meeting, the annual meeting, the attendant dinner, the vote, and, of course, the new role. Further, in those initial weeks, there was a tension inside me. Although I had been running many things as COO, the shift to CEO felt like stepping into uncharted deep waters. Skip, now executive chairman, was still around, and I needed to step up, but I didn't want to come across as a brash newcomer trying to push him aside.

Skip, seeing my hesitancy, took me aside and gave me crucial advice: "You've got this, this is yours now." He imparted wisdom about asserting my position at the head of the table. His encouragement was invaluable as I transitioned into my new role.

Gradually, I found my rhythm and began to develop my leadership style. Skip's leadership was more top-down, which was much needed for the turnaround, and the entrepreneurial challenges and opportunities he had faced. However, my style was about building a team, providing direction, empowering them, and holding them accountable. When executives came to me seeking answers, I would turn it around and say, "You're an executive vice president; this is your domain." I saw high-level associates not as mere implementers, but as leaders responsible for strategizing, bringing opportunities to life, and problem-solving.

While I wasn't steering WSFS in any radically new direction, I did introduce some subtle changes. In addition to sharing responsibilities with many other executives, I made it a point to casually visit WSFS locations more often. Time in the field, engaging with our people—from customers to associates to affiliates—was a priority. These unscripted conversations were invaluable. They allowed me to build genuine relationships over time; and gather real, actionable feedback.

I thought of it as "two-way information sharing," a crucial process for aligning everyone with the company's goals. Sometimes I would simply ask open-ended questions, like: "If you were king or queen of WSFS, what one thing would you change?" or, "When customers leave us, what's the reason they give?" and, "Why do customers come to us?"

Pretty soon, I was getting insightful responses. Sometimes associates touched on little changes that had to be made around their branches or offices, such as programs that didn't make sense, or a quick paint job that was needed. Other times, my team and I would hear about the ways that customer service could improve, or the latest developments at other banks that we should watch.

The most important step in that process, by far, was taking the information back, and doing something with it. When associates could see that their words had an impact, they became more motivated, dedicated, and proud to do their best work for a company that cared equally about them and valued their contributions. Similarly, when customers noticed changes at the bank in response to their feedback, they too felt valued, and were more likely to stick around.

My leadership training at Wharton, and my Executive Leadership master's program at the University of Nebraska, emphasized the importance of asking good questions, listening actively, and taking action. The Gallup organization's approach—the global analytics firm famous for polling, but also for measuring employee satisfaction and productivity—combining good questions and solid data, also resonated with me. When you do both, you create a groundswell that allows the company to improve from all angles. In a lot of organizations, executives just sit in their corner offices and try to run the company with reports. But I believe there's only so much you can do with a report. A report is just data. You need to talk with the people on the front lines, and listen to them, to really know what's going on.

A Major Personal Hurdle

As the months went on, I became more and more comfortable in my new role. I knew it would take me two or three years to really hit my stride, so I tried not to stress too much about the things that were still challenging. But there was one major hang-up I kept having to confront, one that I felt could take me down if I didn't find a way to overcome it: I was a terrible public speaker. Large groups, small groups, intermediate-sized groups—it didn't matter.

I'm not being dramatic; I was really terrible, and terrified. I was caught up in my obsession with perfection, which I'd had since I was a young child. I felt the need to perform, and the pressure of all eyes on me. I prepared, and prepared, and frankly over-prepared. The words had to be correct, they had to be in the right order, there had to be a joke in the beginning, and some kind of deeper message. I read books; I took classes; I went to some famous executive education programs for public speaking. I even got a personal coach. These efforts taught me plenty of tips about how to be better, but I didn't actually *get* much better because I was still hyper-focused on myself, and with perfection.

The result? Invariably, at some point in my speech, I'd make a mistake, and my whole presentation would go downhill in a hurry. I would lose focus and start sweating. My face would turn red from embarrassment, I would get into a doom loop—"Everyone's looking at me, and I'm failing"—and I would do whatever I could to hold it together and get off the stage.

As the promising new CEO of a big company, I knew this flaw could be severely limiting. You have to be able to communicate your goals with confidence, and to motivate people with your message.

Here's the perspective shift that profoundly elevated my capacity for public speaking: I learned that it really wasn't about perfection at all, but about being authentic and connecting with the audience. To me, the most effective public speakers have a human feel and tone—they're not speaking in elegant, flawless logic and sentences, they're expressing themselves naturally. Shifting my mindset from "performance" to "conversation" transformed my approach. I just focused on conveying a good point effectively—regardless of the words. Of course, there had to be some level of polish, and a competent delivery, but I stopped worrying as much about the phrasing and order of things. And, if I forgot something, I just let it go. I started thinking of public speaking opportunities as comfortable conversations on topics about which I was passionate. This mantra was particularly impactful for me.

It wasn't an overnight change, of course. But as I stepped up to more and more podiums, I centered myself on three key principles: comfortable conversation, imparting wisdom, and effectiveness for the audience (over my own desire for perfection). Gradually, I improved my delivery.

It was a first example for me of an MO that I still use today in every big thing I do, personal or professional: Bring the right mindset before you attempt the right skillset. This evolution in my public speaking approach mirrored my growth as a leader. Little did I know, a real test was just around the corner, as the banking sector faced its biggest trial in many generations.

SEVEN | LESSONS IN TRANSITION

By Skip Schoenhals, as told to Brittany Kriegstein. Skip served as CEO of WSFS from 1990 to 2007, and chairman of the bank's board from 1992 to 2017.

When Mark assumed the role of CEO, I was still working full-time at the bank. Out of courtesy, I would attend the staff meetings—which were now Mark's meetings. But even though I technically outranked Mark as the executive chairman of the board, I was there as a participant, not the boss. Everyone else in the room were *his* direct reports.

Our transition was smooth, overall, but the few disagreements we had were instructive. For example, there was one meeting where I felt Mark was being unfair to one of his subordinates, and I stood up for the individual I believed was being wronged. The details of the meeting blur in my memory, but not the aftermath. Within moments, Mark was in my office. He shut the door and said, "You had no right to do that." He continued, "I had a reason for my actions, it was part of a larger strategy, and you overstepped." He was direct and unflinching. I admitted, "Mark, you're absolutely right. It wasn't my place to intervene."

There was one time in particular where he challenged a decision I made. It took major courage on his part, and he was spot on.

WSFS had once owned an automobile leasing company that helped us in the turbulent, lean years of the early '90s. However, as time progressed, it became clear that the CEO of this company did not uphold the values we cherished, particularly in his treatment of people. Further, what had been a strong source of earning strength gradually turned into a considerable earnings drag. We parted with the CEO, and brought in a very capable successor, but analysis still indicated that this business could get much worse within a few years. By continuing to stay with that company, I was behind in addressing this issue with the seriousness it warranted.

Mark knew I was lacking the information, and some of the objectivity, I needed in that moment in order to part ways with that venture. Eventually, quietly, he laid out the case to me. It was very painful, because it was one of those things where we had to decide to shut it down right then, which would be a big earnings hit. But if we did it my way, it was going to bleed us over several years.

He had the courage to say, "Look, we have to deal with this." I was not seeing it clearly until he walked into my office, but a great leader with sophisticated communication skills can bring another leader out of the fog and into a plan for recovery.

The essence of our successful transition lay in the mutual respect we had for each other. Many experts suggest that when a CEO is succeeded, the outgoing CEO should completely step away. We didn't follow that playbook; instead, we worked closely together during the overlap, which proved invaluable.

A New Home for WSFS

Another time Mark and I had different ideas about how to proceed was when we were deciding whether to move the bank into a new building. In my book about my leadership journey at WSFS, I talked about the "hole in the ground"—the company's infamous attempt to build itself a new headquarters in the midst of the financial turmoil of the '90s. That story was well-embedded in the marketplace for years afterward; an unfortunate metaphor for the situation at WSFS at the time.

By the early 2000s, however, WSFS was in a much better place. And with new successes, and a growing flock of associates, it was becoming apparent that the bank's 120-year-old headquarters building at the corner of 9th and Market Streets wouldn't be able to keep up.

While size was one factor, functionality was another. When the building was constructed in the 1880s, banks were run in a very different way. So we had space for customers to come in and interact with retail staff, but everyone else worked in a maze of small back offices separated by walls, which inhibited collaboration. Compounding those drawbacks were the building's outdated HVAC and internal systems, which often broke down and left associates either too hot, too cold, or without essential services. It seemed time for an upgrade.

From a financial point of view, our occupancy cost for that old building was nominal. But replacing the space with modern functionality and amenities was going to bring our earnings down by 5 or 10 percent because the cost of the lease, the refurbishment, and new amenities would be so high.

We really wrestled with the decision. We also had a very special mural in the building: *The Apotheosis of the Family*, an enormous painting commissioned by WSFS in the 1930s, and painted by local artist N.C. Wyeth. I had said from my very early days at the bank, "I don't want to be the president who trashes the mural."

With that in mind, we began to look elsewhere, including into our own portfolio. The bank happened to already have a plot of prominent property at what was known as the "Gateway to Wilmington": the artery into Wilmington from the north, right on Delaware Avenue between Washington and Jefferson Streets. We had acquired it as collateral on a loan that went bad, and we'd been trying to sell it for years. But it was a prime piece of real estate for a company headquarters. As this set of circumstances converged, between 2004 and 2005, I started to look into the possibility of converting the property into a building for WSFS. The best scenario, as I envisioned it, was a modern, multistory tower that would carry the WSFS name and have space for the bank on several floors, but would also be open to other tenants and ultimately owned by an outside real estate company. To sweeten the deal (and clean house), we would also invite that company to buy our historic headquarters on 9th and Market.

The idea got plenty of pushback from longtime associates who didn't like the thought of an open floor plan, and were concerned that a tall new tower with "WSFS" at the top would fly in the face of the scrappy community bank we were at heart.

As CFO, Mark also pushed back hard against my enthusiasm. He wondered what the new building would mean for the bank's performance.

After some debate, we hammered out our thoughts on a train trip to Washington. We agreed on a few important points: The new building would *not* be the fancy lawyer's office with the marble, oak, and the usual stuff imported from Italy—that would send the wrong message. It would be professional and classy; it would set the right tone in terms of aesthetics, but also reflect the plucky spirit of WSFS. There would be no corner offices for executives. The best places would be reserved for associates and customers, and they would be bright, airy, and welcoming.

Once Mark was on board, I felt comfortable going forward, and we moved into the new building in March of 2007. As it turns out, the timing was perfect—besides aligning well with the introduction of the bank's new strategic and cultural initiatives, the move took place just before the financial crisis hit. Soon after our move, we started growing rapidly, and we finally had a place to put the new hires. Even more crucial, though, was the psychological impact of the building on public perception about WSFS. The headquarters quickly came to represent so much more than just a physical space: It was a new strategy, a new ethos, a new culture; and the nucleus of a growing, changing organization.

After the first three or four years, Mark and I looked at each other and said, "This was one of the best decisions we ever made."

Oh, and the mural: Buccini/Pollin, the real estate management company we eventually hired, came up with a very creative way to preserve it. We had a particularly good appraisal on it for about $6 million, and discovered we could remove it and donate it to the Delaware Historical Society, which gave us a significant tax deduction that helped us finance our new space.

Shared Values

Mark and I, though unwavering in our commitment to ethics, approach the concept from divergent vantage points. My moral compass is firmly rooted in Judeo-Christian principles, reflecting a faith that permeates my daily existence, and profoundly shapes my worldview. Mark, while similarly principled, does not share my religious fervor, yet his ethical foundation remains robust, albeit more humanistic.

Despite our different paths, our shared commitment to ethical behavior united us in the quest to define "doing the right thing" in a manner inclusive of all perspectives. WSFS, as a diverse institution, is home to individuals of various religious beliefs, and none at all. It became imperative for us to formulate ethical guidelines that transcended specific religious doctrines. We immersed ourselves in the literature of business ethics, and engaged in rigorous discussions to cultivate a culture of integrity within our workplace.

From this process emerged two fundamental precepts. First, the primacy of the Golden Rule: treat others as one would wish to be treated. Second, an unwavering commitment to ethical conduct, even when choosing the more challenging path seems unnecessary or inconvenient.

There were instances when we faced regulatory infractions—minor transgressions that, though they could have remained undisclosed, presented an ethical dilemma. As a regulated entity, WSFS frequently encountered such issues, often identifying them independently before they were uncovered during official examinations.

One notable example involved the acquisition of a mortgage

company. Shortly after the acquisition, we discovered a regulatory mistake made by the acquired entity. While we were not legally bound to disclose this finding to our regulatory agency, we chose to do so, adhering to our principle of transparency and doing the right thing, regardless.

Initially, the president of the mortgage company was (understandably) taken aback by our decision. Nevertheless, our commitment to "doing the right thing" prevailed, reinforcing our ethical standards and demonstrating our dedication to integrity.

The truth is, Mark is one of the finest leaders I've encountered. During his time at the helm of WSFS, he always looked at what was best for the team, and made sure he had the *right* team—holding the team's results high above individual performance. When I stepped back and let him take the reins, I didn't have to do much. He has humility, and yet he's persistent. When he believes he's right, he's got the courage to stand up to anybody.

EIGHT | WSFS CULTURE TAKES FLIGHT

By Mark Turner

I n the early days of my tenure as CFO, Skip embarked on a thorough exploration of what constituted "culture" within WSFS. To him, culture was not merely a set of norms, but the very ethos that bound our collective efforts: our guiding principles, our playbook, our bible. It was the invisible force that steered us all in a unified direction. Skip was convinced that a deeper cultural understanding was essential for WSFS, and he had become especially interested in the Gallup organization (as mentioned in Chapter 6). Skip believed that Gallup's expertise could pave the way for a more nuanced and distinct company culture.

I, however, was less convinced.

As a relatively green CFO, I harbored doubts about the practical value of culture. How could one operationalize such an abstract, elusive concept? What metrics could gauge cultural "success"? And would its impact on WSFS ever be tangible in terms of cold, hard numbers?

Despite my reservations, I agreed to accompany Skip to a Gallup seminar in Washington, DC. It was a one-day event designed to showcase their research and methodologies. Gallup's approach involved comprehensive surveys and assessments of employees. The data collected was then relayed back to the company, where it fell to management to craft strategies aligned with the findings. Gallup asserted that enhanced employee motivation would manifest in improved operational outcomes, and that a positive culture inevitably yielded quantifiable operational and financial benefits.

The notion intrigued me. Gallup was employing scientific methods—rigorous data, concrete evidence—to enhance workplace conditions and company performance. Gallup's meta-research showed that companies in the top quartile, that had world-class engagement, consistently outperformed others by a factor of 23 percent on the bottom line. That's huge in a competitive environment where a few percentage points can make the difference between high performance or being swallowed up by a stronger rival. On the train on the way back, I told Skip I was sold. "But if we do it, we have to really commit to it. This is a multi-year process."

He agreed: "Let's do it." And at that moment, a new era for WSFS culture was born.

Our Partner Gallup

WSFS' relationship with Gallup actually started before that train ride epiphany. In 1998, Skip decided to run a Gallup survey for the first time—as a response to the belief that it would be good to know what associates were thinking and feeling in the years after the company had been recapitalized and run by new management.

The results were pretty sobering.

The bank's engagement ratio—which calculates the level of engaged associates to actively disengaged associates—was about 1.1 to 1. For context, the national average at that time was around 1.5 to 1. A ratio was considered "good" if it was 4 to 1; a "world-class" ratio was all the way up around 8 to 1. With about half of WSFS associates disengaged and unenthusiastic about their work, it was clear that something had to change—and that it would take time.

And it did take time. In the 15 years after Skip and I agreed to go all in with Gallup, strengthening our core culture was a central focus. WSFS' engagement ratio soared from rock bottom to an astonishing 14 to 1, far surpassing the "world-class" benchmark.

My own transformation was remarkable too. Jacque Merritt, a seasoned leadership coach at Gallup, became my executive coach when I enrolled in the Gallup MBA program at the University of Nebraska, in 2004. Under her guidance, I honed my leadership skills in alignment with Gallup's principles. "Mark was initially skeptical," she recalled. "His analytical nature made him wary of what seemed like a passing trend. His top strength, as revealed by the CliftonStrengths 34 report, was 'Learner'—a deep-seated passion for knowledge and improvement. He was driven more by the learning process than by the outcomes. The second strength was 'Relator,' indicating his profound satisfaction in forming meaningful relationships and working collaboratively. Third was 'Significance,' which meant that Mark sought impactful leadership roles."

Yet these strengths had their drawbacks, she explained. Learners can inadvertently push others to also over-prioritize knowledge-gathering. Relators take time to trust others, so can gravitate too much toward their own inner circle, giving others the impression that they're closed off. Those seeking Significance can be perceived as caring too much about their own reputation, or striving too hard for perfection.

Jacque's work with me focused on identifying and addressing these potential blind spots to enhance my leadership efficacy. And this was crucial: 70 percent of employee engagement hinges on strong managerial leadership. Jacque's coaching; and Gallup's focus on strengths-based leadership, positive psychology, and emotional intelligence had a transformative impact on my leadership.

Jacque noted that "Mark's full adoption of Gallup's approach set WSFS apart, particularly during challenging periods like the 2008–2009 financial crisis and Great Recession," adding that, by that time, "WSFS had already fortified its cultural foundation, rendering it more resilient."

Sheila Hacker joined WSFS in October 2007, as facilitator on the learning and development team. Several years later, her manager recognized her passion for associate engagement and culture, and made her director of that team. She also assumed responsibility for "Human Sigma"—a role we defined as the compounding benefit of associate engagement and customer advocacy. Her partnership with Gallup began then, and flourished over the course of 16 years, until her retirement in 2024. "If we wanted to be a high-performing bank," she said, "we had to have really engaged customers who were willing to spend more, do more, and stick with us through thick and thin. But we also had to have really engaged associates who were willing to work with them. Gallup's research in the field of employee engagement was crucial to us, helping us harness the strengths of our associates while helping to improve our collective weaknesses."

There are 12 factors at the center of Gallup's main questionnaire, basics like "I know what's expected of me at work," "I have the materials and equipment I need to do my work right," and "At work, I have the opportunity to do what I do best every day." When we did a survey, we'd get the results for individual work groups, and then we'd focus on sitting down with that work group and having a conversation. What could we be doing differently that we could own and control, and make our team and the company better?

The associates in that group would collectively come up with a plan to make changes, so they all had ownership over the outcome. That strategy also gave disgruntled or disengaged people an avenue to come on board and have their voice heard. We knew we couldn't have a good service environment unless we attracted the best people, handed them the tools they needed, and gave them reasons to love the company and want to serve our customers. Small improvements each year led to huge improvements over time. Using the same methodology across the organization led to a more unified, and stronger culture.

The results are real. For a hospital that did the same survey, for example, higher engagement meant a lower death rate for patients. That really drove it home. For WSFS, higher engagement meant superior customer care and internal cohesion, ultimately translating into critical results. Now, thousands of companies use these or similar strategies around culture to make associates and customers more engaged—but I think we were very early in trying to implement it fully.

As of this writing, WSFS has received Gallup's Exceptional Workplace Award seven times; has received the local paper's "Top Workplace" designation over 15 times; has been named to Forbes' Lists of World's Best Banks, America's Best Banks, and America's Best Midsize Employers; and has been identified as one of the 50 most community-minded companies in the Pennsylvania, New Jersey, and Delaware region. My team and I were asked to share the story of our partnership with Gallup at panels across the country, and we were featured in articles that highlighted the strength of our culture thanks to these initiatives. Companies like Wawa, DaVita, and Herr Foods Inc. came to WSFS to spend a day learning about our Gallup strategies. We even got a visit from representatives of Westpac Bank in Melbourne, Australia. And every time a company scheduled to visit us, we shared information about that company with our associates, and solicited their insights so we could share their voice with our visitors.

Over time, our bottom-line numbers improved—just as Gallup's meta-research predicted they would—and we became a top quartile bank. The cause and effect were clear and indisputable.

That's just the top of a long, long list of accolades that highlight the effort we put in to make WSFS a great place to work, and a great partner for business. But sustaining and enhancing culture is a daily endeavor; it runs top-down from executive decisions, and bottom-up from every associate's actions. It's small things, like name badges that have our credo on them, or sharing cultural success stories via email; and it's big things, like having the right policies and the right people in the right places. We have had so many exemplars of our culture: people like Shari

Kruzinski, Lisa Brubaker, Justin Dunn, Cheryl Hughes, Karen Allen, Jim Wechsler, Sarah Tracy, Bob Mack, Tom Kearney, Jim and Arlene Lucianetti, Gail Chase, Renny Giovannozzi, Tom Grant, Vernita Dorsey, and Virginia Darnel, all of whom you could count on to do the right thing at the right time; and who always showed some combination of dedication, loyalty, enthusiasm, service, and integrity in everything they did. These people and many others were people you pointed to and said, "*they* are WSFS." They were and are the real stars of our organization.

There's one more character in this chapter of WSFS history—a main character—who was a critical hire when our efforts with Gallup and culture were really starting to build momentum. I quickly realized that we needed someone who could spearhead this campaign—a cultural quarterback, if you will. This had to be someone who'd understand that WSFS' most valuable resources were its associates; someone who truly knew what made folks tick, and how to bring out the very best in them. Her name is Peggy Eddens, and you'll meet her when you turn the page.

NINE | PEOPLE MATTER

*By Peggy Eddens, as told to Brittany Kriegstein. Peggy
was the chief human capital officer and executive vice
president at WSFS from 2007 to 2021, and the primary
driver of WSFS' cultural transformation.*

In 2007, WSFS Bank was a 175-year-old, publicly held company, with strong local ties and a captivating history. I discovered they were on the hunt for an executive vice president and director of human capital, and I felt an immediate and intense connection to the role. It seemed like the perfect opportunity, and I was eager to seize it.

I wanted to stand out, so I wrote Mark a series of handwritten letters to give him a real sense of my extensive experience with culture and people. I included my annual self-review as a sort of show-and-tell, proving that I wasn't just spouting principles, but actually living them.

That summer, Mark invited me to Wilmington for an in-person meeting, and I ended up landing the job—despite a rival candidate from New York with a résumé the size of a small book. I guess Mark just thought I had the right stuff, and if you think about it, a lot of what makes a good director of human capital doesn't come through on paper. We had an easy rapport, something that I think came from a deep sense of shared values.

It didn't take long for me to realize that Mark and I were cut from the same cloth. I was the fourth of five girls with Depression-era parents who always propelled us to reach for a high bar through hard work and education. And just as Mark struggled with public speaking, I went to speech therapy for years to overcome stuttering, starting when I was just two-and-a-half years old.

Despite my achievements—graduating summa cum laude from Robert Morris University and amassing a résumé that showcased my expertise—I was often underestimated, and I was a woman in a man's world. I'll never forget how many past interviewers had asked me, "How many words a minute can you type?" or "Do you do shorthand?" The fact that I was seasoned in accounting, management, statistics, and economics did not seem to register.

It took steady determination to get my first job at Koppers Company, a Fortune 500 corporation headquartered in Pittsburgh that specialized in a variety of industrial products and services. This was 1976. I joined a team of four men as the only female auditor, and, on my very first day, the auditor at the corner desk peered at me over his newspaper and said, "This used to be a fraternity." That was my onboarding.

Hungry for work and experience, I pushed forward, eventually joining the men on audit trips around the country. While they immersed themselves in files and paperwork—payables and receivables, payroll records, inventory reports—I would complete my given tasks and then walk around the plant, talking to the folks who knew best about their particular office, and how it felt to work there. I learned how to earn the employees' trust and confidence, and how to truly listen to what they had to say. Before long, employee perspectives and organizational snapshots evolved to become an important part of the audit report.

My colleagues took notice, and commented on the value I was bringing to the team.

The people skills I was honing would eventually prove crucial for the next steps in my career: After three years with Koppers, I accepted an opportunity to join the Marketing and Communications department at Mellon Bank; and later signed up for evening classes at La Roche University, which offered a Master of Science in Human Resource Management. I was officially a "professional people person."

My career path would wind through a few HR opportunities—most notably a family-owned community bank north of Pittsburgh, which was one of my best and most impactful experiences to that date. But when my son started medical school, I began to look for something new. I wanted to find a publicly held company where I could earn equity. At this point, I had spent enough time in a variety of organizations to know exactly what kind of place my new corporate home needed to be. It wasn't long before I found a company that fit all my criteria and aspirations: about 300 miles away from Pittsburgh, in Wilmington, Delaware.

Planting Seeds, Cultivating Roots

At most banking institutions, the word "capital" refers only to the company's financial holdings and net assets. But WSFS recognized a different kind of valuable capital among its ranks: people. After all, how would the bank function without the folks who turned the gears, and crunched the numbers, and helped the customers each day?

The importance of the associates at WSFS meant that my role soon became so much more than just the head of the Human Resources department. I was given an equally important and descriptive name: chief human capital officer. Everyone was now looking to me to be the strength, spark, and glue behind WSFS' cultural transformation.

One of the first things I did was make a schedule, committing to meet everyone at the company within my first three months. It would be a tall task: I'd have to make my way to, at that time, 35 branches and several additional office locations. There would be hundreds of names to learn and stories to hear. But it was crucial.

In doing that, I learned just how much the associates really loved the company and cared for the organization. They were committed to being valued resources for the community, but in turn, they needed to know that we were interested in their stories and their skills, and that we wanted to learn as much about them as we could. We wanted to be different from other companies, where they'd just be considered employees.

Besides listening with a compassionate ear, I would look around: making sure that everyone was working in safe and comfortable environments. At every location I visited, I made a point to examine the kitchen, the coffee area, and the restroom—vital indicators of safety and comfort. With time, that further evolved into making sure people felt like the office was a home away from home, and their fellow associates were family to them.

Telling the Truth

A lot of this work was exciting and joyous for me, but there were difficult conversations too. At one of our very first meetings, Mark asked me to give him a run-down of associates by the numbers, including diversity and demographics. After looking at the data, I saw the weak spots: there were very few women and minorities at the senior level. I wasn't sure if that was something my new boss wanted to hear.

Thinking back to a piece of advice I'd gotten from an earlier mentor, I looked at Mark and asked, "Do I have your permission to be honest with you?"

He was taken aback. "Of course," he said.

Then I explained that if you took a snapshot of the company with regard to diversity, you'd see that women and minorities were mostly inhabiting lower level roles. "We need to find ways to bring them up, and bring more in."

Mark took it in, appreciative. "You never have to ask my permission to be honest again," he said, and then asked me to get to work improving our senior ranks.

As simple as that conversation sounds, it told me everything I needed to know about Mark as a leader and a human, about what he wanted for the bank, and about the working relationship he expected us to have.

I knew that I'd found a boss who would allow me—and the company—to become the best versions of ourselves through truthfulness, transparency, and hard work. I had to rise to the challenge and show him what I could do.

A Really Good Day

What if every day of work at WSFS was not just good, but uplifting and energizing? That was our goal. We were thinking holistically about our employees' lives, about how they transitioned from the workday to home, and back to work. People are more apt to do the yard work, walk the dog, or coach a little league team if they leave their workday feeling fulfilled. And then, they'll come into work the next morning with energy and a positive attitude.

I soon distilled the pillars of associate life at WSFS into four elements: work, play, learn, and care. We were there to serve— our work was a form of service. But we also wanted to play: we wanted to have fun, laugh, and enjoy our time together. Learning was very important, so we implemented programs for advanced courses, and we rotated our associates into new roles to energize them and open new possibilities for them. Care was reflected in all the work we did for the community, and how kindly we treated each other.

In December 2007, Jen Jurden, a consultant who later joined us as our culture strategist, shared with me the concept of introducing a fictional "spokescharacter" into our organization. That character would be named Jurdy: a witty and engaging green cartoon creature with a huge grin. Jurdy became the voice for our associates as we launched our idea generation initiative, Jurdy Spark, and it remained active for over 15 years—an exceptional record for such a program. We set up a Jurdy e-greetings site on our intranet, so associates could connect and send each other messages for all kinds of things, from birthdays and anniversaries to get well cards to recognition of good work. To date, more than four thousand of those messages have been sent annually, from one associate to another; deepening relationships, forming friendships, and emotionally connecting the workforce.

I know all these things might sound insignificant, or too "squishy" to make much of a difference to the bottom line. But as these simple initiatives were implemented, the results were astounding. Before long, without being asked, our associates would open branches early for the customers waiting by the door; they would bring debit cards to people's homes if they forgot or lost them. They would go above and beyond every day, exemplifying the "We Stand For Service" motto that was like gospel to us. And all we had to do was give them a working atmosphere where they were heard, where they were valued, and where they knew how much we cared for them. As a result, the work felt a lot less like work to them, and a lot more like a vocation, a passion to serve.

Growing Together

Whenever we were asked about our organization, or presented our "WSFS Story," we would always lead by saying that our associates were, and still are, the root of our success. Supporting and bolstering them was what we called our "secret sauce": a recipe that combined culture and values to make a truly special working environment.

Our associates also served as our protectors, or antibodies, repelling the things that sought to weaken our culture, or threaten the health of our organization. As WSFS acquired new companies, this was more important than ever: It was paramount that new associates—sometimes hundreds at a time—would mix in seamlessly, strengthen the organization, and help to carry out our "We Stand For Service" mission.

During my tenure, the bank more than quadrupled in size— from 400 associates to 1,900, and from $2.5 billion in assets to over $20 billion. Without a strong cultural underpinning, the organization could have easily become very disjointed. For that reason, being the cultural leader at WSFS was a significant responsibility: I needed to be all-in, all the time; never doing things halfway, and never resting on my laurels.

Thankfully, Mark was our most vocal and present culture advocate. He defined and lived "who we are," and modeled how we got things done at WSFS. Since he was so supportive, it was not uncommon for my team to tee up ideas for Mark to consider that were untried and unconventional. And I cannot remember a time when he gave us a flat "no." He was always open to our suggestions, and willing to give them a try.

With his blessing, we established a variety of programs and traditions that helped foster a sense of community across the company. Things like the "Chalk Talk" board—where associates and executives alike could write down their ideas and converse— which brought people together. Mark, with his constant emphasis on integrity and collaboration, wrote up one of his favorite sayings as the first message on the board: "Whoever gets to the truth first, wins."

Years later, post-Great Recession, we had our first Founder's Day. If you're familiar with Wilmington, you know that WSFS

sits across the street from Wilmington & Brandywine cemetery—Wilmington's oldest cemetery, and the place where a
number of local luminaries are laid to rest. And we discovered
that WSFS' founder, Willard Hall, was buried there; we could
actually see his grave marker when we looked out our windows.
Coming together as a unit each year, to commemorate Willard
Hall's life and legacy, emphasized our longevity, reverence for
our history, and our ongoing commitment to service. Standing
at his grave, one can look up and see the WSFS Bank sign atop
our corporate headquarters. We often felt that Hall was watching
us, and calling us to uphold all that he valued.

Mark's support, belief in us, and the importance he gave to
culture, allowed me and others to lead with our hearts as we
further embedded our culture across a growing footprint. Our
culture thrived, became the soul of our organization, and set the
foundation for our strategic plans in the coming years. And in
times of great calamity, our culture kept us steady.

TEN | CRISES

By Mark Turner

T he financial earthquake of 2008 was preceded by tremors which were dismissed by most. Even as pundits spoke about a growing bubble in housing that threatened to burst, many responded with, *No, this time is different.*

But by 2007, the signs were abundant, if you looked. For years it had seemed that everyone, everywhere wanted housing—as many homes as possible, bigger and bigger, as fast as they could be built. This was partly caused by the deep consumer desire for "nesting" in the years post-9/11, and the significant support pumped into the system after that shock. Interest rates were brought low. Banks, mortgage companies, and other financial spigots were pouring money into the sector. Construction was booming. People who had very low credit scores could get mortgages, partially encouraged by government policies. And, as prices escalated, novice housing entrepreneurs were buying multiple units with easy mortgages, and flipping them quickly for profit.

Homeowners who weren't buying new homes were tapping the equity in their homes like an ATM, increasing their mortgage balances to build *more* house, beyond what was already there. Developers were borrowing money and paying for land to keep constructing. Builders and contractors with little experience got into the business. Speed of delivery was paramount. Buyers and packagers of mortgage loans demanded more product to sell so they could make easy, quick money, pulling more debt into the system.

Scrutiny and discipline became lax across the board, and fraud and mismanagement ensued. Some borrowers lied about their income to get mortgages. Some developers lied about the progress of their projects or how their loaned money was being spent. Banks were pushing lending concentration limits. Rating agencies were giving imprimaturs—official endorsements—that weren't deserved, to mortgage securities. Regulators were behind the curve, and didn't want to stifle innovation in the housing market. Every part of the supply chain in the housing sector was delusional, greedy, sloppy, or all three. To this day, it's hard to figure out exactly who the prime perpetrators were, versus who were just contributors to the mess. All were complicit.

As always in a party of excess, at some point the libation wears off, fatigue sets in, and the music stops. Regulators started barking, and lenders started getting tighter with the purse strings. Many borrowers who had taken mortgages that they could not afford were unable to refinance, and were defaulting. The developers were in trouble too, as their houses were not being built or selling as predicted. Once those individual mortgages and construction loans started to sour, banks began to suffer, and tighten more—and the downward spiral ensued. So it goes.

As 2007 progressed, and just when I became CEO, the tremors turned into more significant shocks. Most notably, New Century Mortgage, the subprime mortgage giant, went bankrupt that

April; and Countrywide Mortgage, the largest provider of mortgages in the US, unraveled throughout 2007 (and had to be sold in January 2008). In July 2007, a couple of Bear Stearns' subprime mortgage–fed hedge funds burst, their damage amplified by traditional strategies of taking on debt to leverage their returns. Still, some hope abounded. "The problem will be contained to the subprime housing sector" was a common refrain at that time.

The truth started to emerge more clearly in early 2008. Bear Stearns, once a towering figure in Wall Street investment banking—whose stock had traded at a healthy $170 per share as recently as a year before—cracked under the growing strain. On Sunday, March 16th, 2008, the firm was hastily sold to JPMorgan Chase for just $2 a share, in a secret deal orchestrated by the US government. (The sale price was later adjusted to $10 a share, after Bear Stearns' stockholders filed a class-action lawsuit.) Immediately, all eyes started to turn to others that might have similar issues.

Lehman Brothers, a Wall Street investment bank, was now under the microscope. At first, they fought off the critics: On tense earnings calls, they beat back tough analysts and investor questions, and stayed afloat. But the forces of reality caught up. On September 15th, 2008, Lehman Brothers could not hide anymore. The legendary investment bank filed for the largest bankruptcy in US history, after reporting billions in losses. That shocking event was covered live, and extensively, by all major news outlets. Challenges at AIG, Merrill Lynch, Washington Mutual, and Wachovia—among other large, notable names— also emerged, traveling down paths of forced sale, bailout, or failure. The byzantine financial engineering and derivatives underpinning Wall Street, and the intense interconnectedness of the financial system, was fracturing in ways no one had thought was even possible.

Meanwhile, at WSFS...

As the crisis deepened, I knew I had to say something to WSFS associates. Early in October 2008, I collected my thoughts and wrote a three-page memo, reflecting on the past, present, and future of the economy; and where WSFS stood amidst the chaos.

It began: "Today marks, exactly, the one-year anniversary of the current Bear market (with a capital "B") in stocks. And with recent dramatic events on Wall Street and in Washington, and with the market nosedive over the last several trading sessions, this seems like an especially appropriate time to summarize my thoughts on those happenings."

My memo detailed the roots of the crisis—a culture of reckless borrowing, lax lending standards, inadequate risk management and regulation, and an excessive appetite for more. "The economy is officially sick, if not technically in a recession," I wrote.

I had to be honest about the dire situation we were facing, but I also wanted to make clear that for WSFS, there were real reasons for hope. The company had entered the downturn in a strong position, and was holding up well. I listed some of the highlights: a solid and diverse balance sheet, ample funding sources, the absence of large surprise write-offs, strong capital, stable earnings, healthy reserves, and an impending six-branch purchase from rival Sun Bank.

"There may come a time when we get a skinned knee or a bloody nose in this," I wrote. "In fact, we've had a few small ones already. But one thing we should all really, really appreciate is that because of our culture, we have—and will—handle(d) them very well. Think about how engaged our associates and customers are, and how we rise to challenges. Think of the stories of how our front line and support associates have worked together to reassure customers about FDIC insurance, at a very nervous time for them. The combination of our financial strength, noted above, and the cultural strength I just mentioned, puts us far, far ahead of others in handling this economic sickness; and, importantly, in continuing to help our communities and good customers at a difficult time."

I ended the letter by reminding associates that WSFS had been through big storms before, with share prices dipping below $10 as recently as December 2000. "Concerns were different," I said, "but remember that cycles come and go, and as one of the 10 oldest banks in the country, we have seen, and thrived through, more than almost any of them."

How Did WSFS Get Through the Crisis?

Four hundred and eighty-nine FDIC-insured banks failed between 2008 and 2013, during and after the Great Recession. This was a radical increase from the total of 10 bank failures, in the five years prior to 2008. Additionally, hundreds of banks were sold because of general weakness during that period. In all, the US banking industry shrunk by well over 10 percent as a direct result of the financial crisis and the ensuing deep recession.

And yet, when WSFS emerged from this bleak period, we found ourselves stronger than before. Our story is one of wise strategy, prudent risk management, tough and collaborative decisions, and nurtured relationships. These actions, though not always obvious at the time, were what kept the bank on relatively solid ground during turbulent times.

In the early 2000s, Delaware mirrored the nationwide surge in land development and housing. Low real estate taxes and more affordable living was attracting flocks of retirees from mid-Atlantic states like New York, Pennsylvania, New Jersey, and Maryland. As infrastructure evolved to cater to these new residents, the demand for services and housing intensified, drawing even more people and investment into the region.

Simultaneously, Delaware's seaside towns like Lewes, Rehoboth, Dewey, and Bethany, which were shielded from the bad hurricanes that battered Florida and the Carolinas, became highly sought-after locales. This led to a dramatic escalation in land values in southern Delaware, specifically in Sussex County, where farmland prices soared from $5,000–$15,000 per acre to $100,000–$150,000 per acre.

In turn, the rising demand spurred developers to embark on new projects at a breakneck pace. To build clusters of 20, 100, or 200 homes, substantial land acquisition and construction capital were required. Banks, therefore, became central players in this high-stakes game. Initially, this dynamic worked well: land was developed, homes were built and sold, loans were repaid, and profits were made.

WSFS, as a growing Delaware institution, had to stay competitive. However, in the early 2000s, a few seasoned board members, notably then–lead director CG Cheleden, and long-time director Joe Julian, began to recognize the signs of a brewing bubble. They wisely cautioned against the unchecked exuberance: *We've seen this movie before, and it doesn't end well.*

What followed was a rigorous process of analysis and dialogue. With pushback from those managing bank relationships and sales—those who feared that limiting loans would leave WSFS trailing behind competitors and jeopardize our reputation—a consensus was reached. The solution was to continue to participate, but impose strict lending limits. Development and construction loan limits were carefully structured around percentages of capital and percentage of total loans; they also limited amounts to a specific borrower, county, and project exposures. This ensured that the bank was not too exposed while still supporting our customers and the market.

Between 2004 and 2008—and after—the bank's board and management demonstrated remarkable discipline. At the time, these measures may have seemed overly cautious or even restrictive. Yet, in retrospect, they were a crucial safeguard, shielding WSFS from the huge mistakes that ensnared many of our peers.

In contrast, Wilmington Trust, our big, nearby competitor, increased its lending aggressively, often nearing legal limits and partnering with developers of questionable standing. When the housing bubble inevitably burst, Wilmington Trust was left grappling with numerous large, failed projects and substantial losses.

The ability to stand firm amidst widespread enthusiasm was a key factor in our eventual success. Furthermore, understanding mortgage risk from our many prior ventures, and exiting them at the right time, prevented WSFS from succumbing again to the allure and pain of exotic mortgages. In 2008, when these high-risk assets were wreaking havoc across the financial landscape, our exposure was manageable.

Importantly, we also avoided investing in the troubled stocks of Fannie Mae and Freddie Mac—housing finance giants that were subsequently nationalized, and saw their bonds plummet to worthless levels. Moreover, we steered clear of investments in trust-preferred securities, which were bonds issued by other banks that were hit extremely hard in the financial turmoil.

Finally, the early part of our new strategy focused on organic growth—proving we had something of value to sell to individual customers before acquiring large quantities of customers—and therefore we avoided the pitfalls of over-priced mergers and acquisitions. Many banks that had completed big acquisitions at inflated prices faced steep declines in those asset values on their books. By contrast, WSFS' minimal engagement in these aggressive areas meant that we were spared the need for significant asset write-downs or write-offs.

Ultimately, WSFS was forced to deal with problem development loans, as every bank did who participated in the market of the preceding decade. However, our issues were localized in one area of our balance sheet, so it was painful, but not debilitating or deadly.

Another crucial element of our strategy, one that proved invaluable during the crisis, was our approach to media relations. Recognizing the potential for negative headlines to destabilize our position, I established a strategic rapport with local reporter Eric Ruth.

Eric was new to the business and banking beat. I saw an opportunity to provide him with deeper insights into the complexities of the banking world, and the impending financial storm. This relationship was not just about information exchange; it was about building trust, open communication, and faithful representation.

We spent time together over several lunches, getting to know each other beyond the surface level. This personal connection was essential. By fostering a strong, authentic relationship, I helped ensure that, should any issues arise at WSFS, Eric would have a reliable channel to seek clarification and get the full, true story.

When the crisis did unfold, our proactive engagement with Eric paid off. His reporting was measured and thoughtful, free from sensationalism. Even as WSFS faced challenges and reported adverse results, Eric's coverage remained balanced and informed. His ability to delve into the nuances, and present a well-rounded view, helped avoid mistaken or alarming headlines, preserving the market's stability and our reputation in a turbulent time.

A Timely Return

As a leader, I've always believed in the art of "managed transparency": the idea of being as forthcoming with my staff as possible, without letting everyone in on every stray concern running through my mind—which were many at this fraught time. Outwardly, I tried to exude my overall confidence in WSFS. But inwardly, I certainly was worried: as CEO of a beloved community bank during this tenuous period, it was impossible not to be.

As the economic turmoil reached a crescendo, the anxiety among bank regulators rose to a fevered pitch. Our primary overseer, the Office of Thrift Supervision (OTS), escalated its scrutiny, imposing a Memorandum of Understanding (MOU) on WSFS, and other stringent regulatory measures on many financial institutions. These regulatory actions were more than mere formalities, they were binding agreements that held our board and management accountable for implementing corrective actions to steer clear of disaster. While the need for compliance was evident, the sheer volume of requirements quickly became an overwhelming internal focus.

What kept me awake at night, however, was the dramatic decline in our bank's stock price. It had plummeted from a recent high of $65 per share to a troubling $16 in March 2009. I was deeply concerned that if it fell further, particularly below $10, panic would set in. This could trigger a cascading effect—depositors might withdraw their funds in droves, potentially setting off a catastrophic downward spiral that would be difficult to reverse, leading to the bank's demise.

Amidst this precarious situation, a critical figure from WSFS' past reemerged. Ted Weschler, a former investor and board member who had stepped down in 2007, re-entered the scene as a pivotal investor. Ted believed in the bank's true value, so he purchased a substantial amount of our stock on the open market in early 2009, when it was falling into the teens. This decisive action was instrumental in halting the precipitous slide in our stock price. It's hard to overstate the significance of his intervention—without it, we could have seen our stock fall into single digits, potentially triggering a run on the bank.

Ted's commitment to WSFS didn't end there. In addition to the nearly $25 million worth of stock he purchased in the open market, he purchased another $25 million in stock a few months later, in the form of a Private Investment in Public Equity (PIPE). Those transactions quickly made Ted the largest owner of the company, with about 20 percent of its shares. To the market, this was a huge vote of confidence in WSFS, our team, and me, and from a savvy investor to boot. Besides stabilizing us with his investments, Ted's investigative process during his PIPE due diligence helped our team recognize and act on some crucial concerns that we didn't see to be as problematic as they were. Ted highlighted a sobering reality, noting "I believe things are going to get worse for you, and for the entire industry—2009 will probably be a year of losses."

I've come to think about Ted's actions then as a kind of philanthropic capitalism. He gave his time, talent, and treasure over many years, in order to better WSFS, and the lives of many people. He also did so rightly expecting that he would get the financial residue of these good works, and as WSFS and its communities prospered, Ted did extremely well on his investments. But it cannot be overstated: Ted's courage and timely stock purchases in 2009, along with his later return to the board, were not merely pecuniary decisions—they were a lifeline that helped us survive one of the most turbulent periods in banking history.

Troubles in Our Backyard

One October morning in 2008, in the thick of the financial crisis, we glanced out our windows to see a long line of people snaking around a TD bank branch just two blocks away. We knew those people weren't waiting for free ice cream or a T-shirt giveaway.

No, it was the makings of a run on the bank: one of several major calamities that would involve our competitors in the marketplace during this time.

The cause of this distress was a systems conversion: TD, a Canadian institution, had recently acquired local Commerce Bank, and as they were changing over systems that weekend, their customers' account balances were not being reflected correctly. So folks were signing into their profiles and seeing the wrong amounts. At such a tumultuous time for the economy and the banking industry overall, panic set in. When people are concerned that their money isn't safe, they come to their bank and ask hard questions, often demanding to withdraw it all. While it's not a big deal if just a handful of customers do that, thousands of withdrawal requests at once can sink a bank almost overnight (as showcased by the stunning failures of Silicon Valley Bank and Signature Bank in 2023).

Looking more closely at the assembling crowd, we noticed something adding to the chaos: A neighboring bank, PNC, had some hastily made signs in their windows that said something like, *Concerned about your banking account? We are here for you, please stop in.* At the same time, nearby Citizens Bank employees were working the line of stressed TD customers who were waiting to go into the bank—handing out new account kits, and encouraging them to switch.

These were short-sighted, low blows; competitive moves that would serve to cause more fear in the marketplace as a whole. Banks are part of a critical, intertwined system; and in 2008 and 2009, we had to stick together, not try to pull each other apart.

I called a quick meeting to decide what to do, and it didn't take long for the team to pinpoint the best course of action. We learned this was now happening at many local TD branches. We asked our associates from our nearby branches to take off their name tags, go over to the TD branches, and ask their employees how we could help. Our associates stepped up, mingled in the lines, quelled concerns, and did triage. Sure, we could have benefitted, marginally, by sucking in some panicked TD customers. But we knew that helping TD at that time also helped the broader market *and* WSFS—calming fears while also creating a feel-good story, and boosting our team spirit, which would elevate our culture and reputation in the long run.

We were right. Our collaborative actions that day became a lesson recounted in books and articles, and fostered strong camaraderie with TD. Most importantly, for us, it became folklore; told and retold within the organization, helping propagate our special culture.

A Major Market Explosion

These events pale in comparison to the shock and reverberations we felt while watching the slow fall of Wilmington Trust, with whom we'd always had a sibling-like rivalry. While we were small and scrappy; they were larger, polished, and elegant; the institution of choice for the legendary DuPont family, and the place where the upper echelons of Delaware society would store their fortunes. I called them the 800-pound gorilla in our marketplace.

From their tall headquarters just a few blocks away, it often felt like they looked down on WSFS, seizing on the fact that we almost failed ingloriously in the early '90s to intimate that people ought not bank with us. In a particularly aggressive jab, they used a law change in 1996 to try to steal our customers by charging them usage fees at ATMs that both banks had always shared— unless our customers switched these accounts to them.

But there were so many chapters to our long relationship. When WSFS was in dire straits during Skip's early tenure as CEO, Wilmington Trust stepped up as a backup investor to keep WSFS from failing. It was a nice gesture, but I think for Wilmington Trust there was also some self-interest at play—as in, they would rather see us stick around as a weaker bank, than have a bigger, stronger bank come in, buy us, and compete with them.

No matter how you look at it, WSFS and Wilmington Trust were both important parts of the Delaware banking ecosystem. So, when we started seeing them do increasingly risky development lending in the early-to-mid aughts, we were concerned. As we scaled back some of our real estate lending, Wilmington Trust confidently continued to make large loans to their customers— especially the ones who were building housing developments downstate, in former farmland near the beaches. By that time, savvy marketplace experts were already starting to see the writing on the wall. In retrospect, it's clear that Wilmington Trust was making dangerous decisions.

In 2010, things came to a sudden and shocking head for our "big brother." One Friday that October, Wilmington Trust's stock price plunged to a shocking $8, down from a peak of near $45 a share a few years earlier. To prevent the regulators from assuming control, Wilmington Trust had no choice but to sell—and sell fast. In a dramatic "take-under" that unfolded over the weekend, they were bought for a meager $3.84 per share by M&T bank, based in Buffalo, New York. Clearly, the situation had been desperate.

Unfortunately, the sale was not the end of the troubles that had come to roost at Wilmington Trust. M&T, to support the price it paid, would have to cut jobs, eventually putting hundreds of local people out of work. What's more, some of the bank's once-mighty executives were brought low by criminal allegations that they had deceived investors, the government, and local community members about how bad their problems really were. Some of the charges were thrown out after years of trials and appeals, but some of the executives were eventually convicted, and some even served jail time.

While the sale came as a major shock to the wider marketplace, we weren't surprised. Many other companies in our position probably would have gloated, but instead of feeling triumphant, I felt saddened by the loss. A large, local, important institution was gone, taking with it valuable jobs and significant wealth. And although they caused us competitive headaches, Wilmington Trust ultimately challenged us to be a better company. Their demise was not something to be happy about.

At once, I put together a memo to all of our associates, setting the tone: *With a big brother, you follow them, you learn from them, you admire them, you annoy them, and one day, when the time is right, after having suffered many a beating from them in all manner of rivalry, you hope to surpass them in a fraternal way. Through the years, I think we can claim many of those same things with our relationship with our big brother, Wilmington Trust.*

I made it clear that engaging in schadenfreude wasn't right, and wasn't us. However, it was our obligation to step up and serve where they couldn't anymore—and become a better institution in the process. We welcomed many of Wilmington Trust's discarded employees, evaluating their potential not just for their skills, but for their ability to bounce back from their tough experiences. As an organization, we asked: Is this person's potential worth the risk? Do they acknowledge their part in the bad situation? Can they genuinely articulate what they would do differently next time? Do they have foundational character to grow through their failures? The people who answered those questions well were at a crucial inflection point of learning, growth, and proving their true worth, and we wanted them at our bank.

In both instances—the mini–bank run at TD and the Wilmington Trust collapse—our actions were guided by a commitment to high standards, our part in the banking system's stability, and the community's health. We navigated these challenges not merely as business opportunities but as tests of our character and values.

ELEVEN | RESPONSE TO CRISES

By Mark Turner

With the economy tanking and markets in a tailspin, government officials were tasked with the near impossible: taming the flames of financial panic before it became an all-out wildfire. Central to this endeavor was a stark realization: The government faced a critical challenge in addressing the toxic assets burdening the balance sheets of America's largest banks. The path forward was fraught with complexities—direct purchases of these bad assets would lead to murky, uncharted territory, while options to sell them off or make them vanish were equally unviable. Instead, the solution lay in a bold injection of billions into the financial system, a move that would both bolster the banks, and establish some government oversight until the storm passed.

As WSFS navigated the turbulence, the imposition of the Troubled Asset Relief Program (TARP) became a significant challenge. Born out of the financial chaos of October 2008—when Lehman Brothers' collapse threatened to unravel the entire economy—TARP aimed to stabilize the situation by injecting capital into major banks.

To put the plan into motion, Secretary of the Treasury Henry Paulson, Federal Reserve Chairman Ben Bernanke, and

then-President of the Federal Reserve Bank of New York Timothy Geithner set up a weekend meeting in Washington, in October 2008, gathering the CEOs of the nation's largest financial
institutions. The message was clear: A big, splashy systemic solution was imperative. The program's mechanics were laid bare,
with financial investments ranging from $5 billion to $15 billion
per institution. And there would be no negotiating. They essentially said: *You have till the end of the day to accept this. So go back
to your boards and get approval.*

Of course, the big banks weren't used to being under the
government's thumb. Some CEOs were flustered by the direc-
tive; others were appalled. Chairman Dick Kovacevich of Wells
Fargo was angry; at first rebuffing the "offer." Years later, in an
interview with CNBC, he'd call the creation of TARP one of the
"worst decisions in the history of the United States."

The urgency of the situation, and the government's weight,
left the banks with little recourse. By day's end, the administra-
tion was poised to reassure the public, declaring that billions had
been allocated to protect both the financial system, and support
wider public confidence.

As the initial program gained traction, medium-sized banks
began to inquire whether they, too, might receive a similar boost.
If they didn't, there would be a flight of customers to the bigger
banks, hastening the possible demise of smaller banks and wors-
ening the "too big to fail" perceptions that the government wanted
to avoid. Thus, a "round two" was devised, tailored for institutions
like WSFS. Unlike "round one," this iteration was more volun-
tary—a factor that introduced a new layer of complexity.

For us and others, the introduction of TARP presented

a dilemma. Accepting the funds risked signaling weakness, while declining them could suggest that we weren't a robust enough bank to qualify. And what if we had a problem down the line? There was still a lot of uncertainty in the air. If we didn't accept them now, would we wish we'd have taken the money after all?

On principle, some of the medium-sized and smaller banks steadfastly refused to accept the TARP money. In some cases, they viewed their decision as a badge of honor; in other cases, they genuinely didn't need the funds. After much deliberation, internally and with regulators, WSFS chose to participate, accepting $53 million. This decision was driven not only by a need for security, but also by a desire to be part of the system's solution.

There were significant drawbacks, and much of it stemming from one line in the contract that essentially said: *We're the US government, and we can change the rules whenever we want.* All we could do was hope the government didn't have any other agenda.

And then they changed everything.

Dodd-Frank

Politicians, acutely aware of the public outcry, found themselves grappling with a critical question: How could we transform the system to avert such crises in the future? In this context, Senator Christopher J. Dodd of Connecticut, and Representative Barney Frank of Massachusetts, emerged as key architects of a bold proposal—one that many viewed as a potential remedy for the ills plaguing the financial landscape. Their collaboration was intended not just as a response to a crisis, but as a decisive move toward a more resilient and accountable financial framework.

The sprawling legislation that emerged, The Dodd-Frank Wall Street Reform and Consumer Protection Act, was more than two-thousand pages of banking legislation and regulation which imposed rigorous standards on the banking industry. It established a few key provisions that had a resounding impact across the American banking world, including additional monitoring and oversight; more education and paperwork about the reality of mortgages for people signing up for them; transparency requirements from lenders; limits of investments, trading, and relationships with private equity firms; more stringent guidelines for credit ratings; a powerful new consumer financial regulator; and expanded protections for whistleblowers.

"This reform will help foster innovation, not hamper it," said President Obama in an address when he signed the act into law in July 2010. "It demands accountability and responsibility from everyone. It provides certainty to everybody, from bankers to farmers to business owners to consumers. And unless your business model depends on cutting corners or bilking your customers, you've got nothing to fear from reform."

That *sounded* good, but banks choked on Dodd-Frank, almost from the beginning. Many felt the legislation was hasty, sloppy, burdensome, and partly misplaced; putting emphasis on the political optics instead of finding truly effective solutions.

Dodd-Frank had a massive ripple effect over financial institutions throughout the country—not just the big, hulking banks it had been primarily crafted to regulate. For one thing, it got rid of the Office of Thrift Supervision (OTS), the primary regulator for many small and medium-sized institutions like WSFS. We'd now have to report to the Office of the Comptroller of the Currency (OCC)—a much larger, more bureaucratic, rigid, and rigorous regulatory agency.

Dodd-Frank also enforced a host of additional responsibilities and requirements on bigger banks, like mandatory bank stress tests, living wills, liquidity stipulations, and capital buffer requirements.

Some of the measures were significant hurdles for smaller and medium-sized institutions, who were tight on resources and still just trying to survive.

Furthermore, the measures piled on a number of restrictions that TARP had already put in place: regulations about how banks spent money; mountains of paperwork to show exactly how the banks were utilizing their government capital; strict limits on executive compensation, expenses, and severance. Sure, it was right to ensure that banks were using their new capital to support their customers. But as the complexities of the situation unfolded, new practical challenges came to light. How could banks responsibly manage severance payments when the requisite restructuring inevitably led to the layoff of employees who were not at any fault for the crisis? The reality of having the government as a business partner introduced an inherent tension, and navigating the landscape of difficult decisions while adhering to government constraints created a fraught operating environment. The daily challenge was striking the balance between accountability and operational flexibility.

It also felt unfair. We had joined the TARP program convinced that we were doing the right thing, playing our part in stabilizing the system. But suddenly, we found ourselves painted as an offender in a narrative we didn't write.

Sleepless Nights

By this point, my work life started to feel like a game of dodgeball—shots coming from every direction that I had to duck or catch. Even if all went well with our new regulations, WSFS could still fail based only on how customers were *feeling*. In the past, bank runs looked like that famous scene in the Frank Capra movie, *It's a Wonderful Life*: masses of people showing up at teller counters with balled fists and anxious eyes. A mini-run on WSFS actually occurred during the early days of Skip's tenure, which is why associates had stationed armored trucks full of cash near some of the branches. But the bank "runs" of today, in a post-internet and now mobile device world, move much faster—all people have to do is "run" to their keyboards and smartphones and demand withdrawals online. Rumors and worry can travel at the speed of light, and withdrawals can take seconds.

During the crisis, we, like everyone else, started experiencing credit concerns which led to fears. In late 2008, and up through 2011, I had almost daily meetings with people in finance and treasury, scenario-planning about our liquidity situation, and testing where we'd get funds if we needed cash fast. Even though we were stable, a bad headline could sink us more quickly than we might be able to respond.

Skip had his fair share of terrifying moments when he first took over the company in the early '90s—like when the bank found itself $70 million short of regulatory capital, and was almost shuttered by federal regulators. (Skip writes about that roller-coaster ride in his book, *From Failing to Phenomenal*). While he was certainly worried, he leaned hard into his Christian faith, which gave him a sense of reassurance that saved him from having too many sleepless nights.

I was not able to cope that way. I couldn't shake the idea that WSFS could fail. It had happened all around us to others, even those we previously thought of as rock solid. Thousands and thousands of customers and families were relying on me, and being reliable was a huge part of my identity. Would I let them all down?

At some point, the relentless anxiety I was managing (or mismanaging) culminated in a bout of extreme insomnia. I could not sleep, hard as I tried. Anyone who's ever experienced this, lying in bed knowing that you have to sleep—that your body needs sleep, but it won't sleep—understands that it is physically, emotionally, spiritually, mentally, and viscerally anguishing.

The worst episode lasted for a couple weeks. I'd sleep for a couple hours or not at all. I was at the point where I was very close to being hospitalized for lack of sleep and its consequences—my body and mind were giving out. The thing I regret most is taking out my fried nerves and short temper on the people I cherished most—my wife and my kids. I am forever grateful for the grace and love they showed me during this most difficult time of my life.

It was only through methodical self-care, including resuming running (my longtime source of strength and solace), and seeking professional help, that I began to reclaim my health and sanity. It was the first time in my life that I saw a psychiatrist and accepted that I would need sleep and anxiety medication. I wish I'd sought help sooner: Just being able to talk to someone about the things that were keeping me up at night was incredibly productive.

What keeps people from seeking professional psychiatric care when they clearly could benefit from it? In my case, I think it was a mix—I was probably influenced by longstanding cultural stigmas about mental illness that associate it with weakness and failure, especially for men. I also didn't think I had the time in my schedule to deal with it. We're all pressed for time—but a real breakdown, which is where I was headed, would have been monumentally more time-consuming and punishing to myself, and everyone around me. Catching a breakdown in the early stages is the best way to save time and harm.

In addition to professional help, there were a few WSFS directors that I relied on for sound advice, support, and compassion at that critical moment. J.J. Davis, Anat Bird, and Ted Weschler were all around my age and stage of life, and each had prior similar personal or professional experiences. Hearing about their trials, and ways to cope, were invaluable in my recovery.

That brutal period was an inflection point in my life. I now have great empathy for other people going through similar torture, whatever the reason. I more easily recognize the symptoms in others, and lend an ear and a hand. When I go on speaking engagements, I have another way I might relate to ambitious, harried professionals. I also feel that if I was able to get through that intense, fractious period, there is almost nothing I can't handle.

TWELVE | REFLECTIONS ON RISK AND PERSEVERANCE

By Ted Weschler, as told to Brittany Kriegstein. Ted was a key WSFS board member and investor who served from 1992 to 2007, and then again during a pivotal time from 2010 to 2013. Ted joined Berkshire Hathaway in 2012, where he works directly with Warren Buffett as one of the firm's two investment managers.

When I left the WSFS boardroom in 2007, I didn't think I'd come back.

But just three-and-a-half years later, I found myself in the building again. The country's financial climate had begun to improve, with banks scrambling to get out of TARP—the Troubled Asset Relief Program—as quickly as they could. It was like the proverbial roach motel: After you got in, it was really hard to escape.

In order to get out from under TARP, WSFS had to pay back the government's loan. But even their efforts to do that were mired in bureaucratic rules: The bank's capital was restricted, and regulators had a say in when and how the bank could use it to repay the loans. To help raise those funds, Mark and his team came back to me and said, "Do you want to invest in the bank again?"

I only took a few days to think it over. With 15 years already under my belt in the WSFS boardroom, I felt like I knew the ins and outs of the company. Skip, and the rest of the board leadership team, took a chance on me back in 1992, as the 30-year-old co-founder of a private equity firm called Quad-C. When we became lead investors in WSFS, I was given the opportunity to fill a seat in that boardroom—and it was an experience that would go on to shape the rest of my career.

As a member of the executive committee, I'd been at the table when they decided to approve some of their biggest loans; I remembered the quality of those conversations, the discipline and care WSFS leadership employed when making those big moves. Even after I became less involved in the day-to-day at WSFS, I still followed the bank closely to keep tabs on the smaller investment I personally had with them. I knew they'd worked hard to build a solid relationship with their community, and I had watched as that community stuck by them when times got tough. Those people were unlikely to pull their money out in a hurry if they caught wind of a bad headline, and that was reassuring.

I had graduated from Wharton, but what I learned from Skip, CG, and the others was, in my opinion, the best real-life education in the industry. Those guys took me under their wings and taught me how to challenge, innovate, ask the tough questions, and make the hard decisions. They taught me what highly effective leadership looks like, and how a group of dedicated, diverse board members can come together to achieve something far beyond what each of them could do alone.

I loved being on the board with them, and when it finally came time for me to leave in 2007, after 15 years, I was sad. But by then, all the stock had been distributed to my shareholders, and

I had my hands full running my own business, Peninsula Capital. It was the right time.

And then, just a few years later, the banking world went through a major upheaval, and WSFS needed help. I'm told I tolerate more risk than most people do, but I wouldn't say that I chase risk. As somebody who runs a portfolio, I have the advantage of not wagering my whole career on any one position. The investment that I would make in WSFS was probably about 5 percent of the fund that I managed—so I wasn't betting the farm, so to speak, but I was still taking a leap of faith. Knowing the institution as well as I did, being able to negotiate a fair price, and being offered a sweetener deal in the form of warrants in the company—a clause that gave me the right to purchase more shares of stock in the company at a predetermined price after a defined numbers of years—all made it sound like a solid investment. I still had a soft spot for WSFS in my heart, and decided to take that plunge to help the bank back onto its feet.

Another factor that made the transaction smoother and quicker than most was that I didn't need approval from my investors; only from regulators who were already well familiar with me and my work. They knew I wasn't a bad actor—and that I was a credible investor whose whole career revolved around accurately assessing risk and reward.

Using the TARP guidelines to come up with a fair price for our transaction, we cut a quick deal in the form of a PIPE—a Private Investment in Public Equity. Because PIPEs have less stringent regulatory requirements than initial public offerings (IPOs), they save companies time and money, and help raise funds more quickly. They also come with the stipulation that the investor must hold the shares for a much longer period of time; shares bought under a PIPE are not immediately tradable like they are after an IPO. So there was the expectation that I'd be sticking around for at least a couple of years, especially with those warrants thrown in. As part of the agreement, I came back onto the board.

A Different World

It took no time at all for me to figure out that the post-crisis boardroom was a much different place than the one I'd left a few years earlier.

So much had changed—both within WSFS and outside its walls. Everybody in banking in that '08, '09 period felt like they went through a near-death experience: The entire system had come close to collapsing, and anyone without a lot of capital was in big trouble. While the WSFS of the early 2000s was willing to take more risks, the WSFS of '08 and '09 was hardened and cautious: especially where shareholders were concerned. A lot of new board members had come on, and the dynamic had totally changed.

The reality is: If you have 15 people sitting around the table, there's a tendency to go with the least common denominator in terms of risk tolerance. The most conservative person at the table can set the tone for the whole institution. There were several folks I would characterize as smart business executives, but they would always see how things could go wrong. They were a bit older, and, as you get older, there tends to be a strong desire for risk avoidance—a tendency to mitigate any and all risks that people are exposed to.

It was a tricky tightrope to walk for an investor like me, who was always seeking to push boundaries for the benefit of WSFS stockholders. I definitely remember a few tense discussions. One such episode unfolded not long after I came back, when the bank had the option to raise additional equity by selling more stock. Several of the board members were of the mindset that more equity would be better—reducing the risk that there would be a regulatory problem down the line. But my view was that selling more stock would dilute my ownership and the ownership of other shareholders. We were already generating additional equity by earning money every quarter, and adding more outside equity at that time just didn't seem like the right thing to do. If we kept making moves to reduce risk, we'd dissipate the potential upside associated with the equation.

As I watched Mark straddle the rift in the boardroom, I could see how difficult it was for him. In many ways, Mark and I were very alike: similar in age and life stage, with similar levels of experience in our respective careers. He didn't have that expertise yet in juggling a big group of people, and I could tell he was trying to find his way. How do you tee up ideas and get consensus from a bunch of very different board directors? How do you get everyone rowing in the same direction, with the same intensity? Mark had tons of experience interacting with regulators, but this was a different story. He had to get comfortable with the fact that he wasn't always going to get exactly what he wanted. You can have 15 people on a board, but it only takes one of them to destroy the whole dynamic. And as a CEO, it's hard to change that, because at the end of the day, the board members are his or her bosses.

Given my perspective on risk and my extensive prior history with the WSFS board, I felt like I was in a unique position to be a supportive voice for Mark. As the biggest shareholder at the bank, I could use that gravitas to make points and open new conversations. We ended up having a healthy open dialogue about the equity issue, and in retrospect, I'm not sure the same conclusions would have been reached if I hadn't been in the room. Skip, who had a lot of his net worth tied up in the bank, was also a helpful ally. We both were aligned in our enormous respect for Mark, and in our belief in his ability to get things done the right way.

Those of us on the board who worked at different companies very quickly understood that WSFS was not like other organizations. University of Virginia COO Jennifer "J.J." Davis served on the board at the same time I did, and often reflected on what made WSFS unique. "WSFS zigs when others zag," she observed. "That is part of WSFS' secret sauce. It tries to do the right thing, the hard thing, in the wake of adversity."

Yes, we did encounter a fair amount of adversity in that room as the crisis continued to shake out across the banking world. But as J.J. said, the way the bank handled itself spoke volumes about the kind of place it was at its core.

"WSFS just is different." J.J. has said. "Its North Star is different, and it sets us apart. And there's such humility—you have CEOs of major companies sitting in the boardroom. It's beautiful and rare. You just wish the rest of the world could be like that."

Looking Back

My second stint on the WSFS board lasted until 2013, when the company issued a proxy, and I didn't stand for reelection. By that time, I had been at Berkshire Hathaway for almost two years, and my plate was getting very full working closely with Warren Buffett. While I was sad, once again, to close another chapter with WSFS, I was invigorated by the transformation I saw in Mark as a leader.

When he was first elevated, he was a very capable guy, but in unfamiliar territory. I'd felt the same way at my first ever WSFS board meeting—I was basically just a kid surrounded by seasoned bankers, decades older; stared down by somber oil paintings of the bank's past leaders. What could I possibly offer to the room that would be helpful?

Over time, we both learned a ton. And I think we went through a lot of the same journey. In that first year on the board, I would freeze up while trying to say something, and I know Mark also battled his own demons with public speaking. As the years went on, I learned how to confidently express my opinions, and Mark became a truly great speaker who had this way of conveying deep knowledge with a lot of empathy to whoever he was talking to. He went from being a controller, which is a pure managerial position, to mastering a broad spectrum of leadership skills. In the CEO role, he learned how to interface with his investor base, community leaders, the board, associates of the company, and customers of the bank. There was more and more public speaking involved, and Mark got better and better at that. In the board meetings during our later years, he'd effortlessly take the reins and manage the agenda. The little things that would have thrown him off in the beginning became white noise that he knew how to overcome.

He also learned—and this is a tough one—how to take criticism. When Mark first jumped into the CEO role, I think he had some understandable trepidation about that. One of the best practices of good corporate governance says that the CEO needs to leave the room for a few minutes during every meeting, to give the board members a few minutes to critique his work. It makes sense in theory, but in reality it's pretty awkward. In my experience, creating that window for board members to talk opened the door to a lot of criticism that wasn't always productive. If they were going to criticize, why not do it *in front* of the CEO, and have a meaningful conversation about it?

In my first several executive sessions, I could tell that the whole process was uncomfortable for Mark. If the critiquing lasted more than five minutes, I'd say, "Look, we have a CEO who's sitting alone in another room. If we have so much criticism for him, shouldn't we just tell him to his face?"

Over time, Mark got used to taking criticism. In the years I was off the board, he evolved meaningfully on that hard skill. I viewed it as an important leadership trait—if you want to run a big company, you really have to be at ease with taking and addressing criticism. Mark became a true leader.

When I was leaving, I knew: *He's got this.* Mark had learned to juggle his hectic schedule with the needs of the board, and had figured out how to make some tough decisions to make that team better. The board was now 100 percent behind him, boasting some great energy to tackle future challenges. His executive team worshiped him, and he also made himself available to everyday associates at the company.

It was an amazing, full-circle moment—especially since I'd seen the bank go through so much over the years. But Mark never got arrogant, even when he met with success. He said, "Let's just roll up our sleeves and get this done."

Mark on the left, Steve and Matt with their mother Helen, 1965.

Helen, Jack and all nine Turner siblings on Camac Street, 1967.

The Turner home on N. 5th Street
near Lehigh Avenue in Philly, 1955-1966.

The Turner home at 5315 N. Camac Street, Philly, 1966–1980.

Mark and Regina at their wedding with best man Steve Booth, 1992.

Frederick Stone's portrait at WSFS.

WSFS Financial lands two new executives

Bank fills spots left empty after attempted sale

By JOSEPH N. DISTEFANO
Staff reporter

WSFS Financial Corp. has hired a former MAC card executive and a controller at the former Meridian Bancorp. to fill senior posts left vacant since the Wilmington banking company was nearly sold last winter.

Thomas E. Stevenson, a veteran of 30 years at the MAC automatic teller system and its predecessors, is now serving as the first-ever

Thomas Stevenson   Mark Turner

chief information officer at WSFS. The company, which owns Wilmington Savings Fund Society, is Delaware's second-largest independent bank after Wilmington Trust Corp.

Stevenson, who was in charge of quality control before leaving MAC, joined WSFS with a man-

date to unify the various computer systems that support WSFS's mortgage, consumer and commercial banking businesses.

His technical responsibilities were formerly handled by WSFS retail banking chief Gordon Dyott, who quit last winter to join a bank in Bloomington, Ind.

Dyott's job was split after his departure. The bank has yet to name a manager to take over his former retail banking responsibilities, but will probably do so before Christmas, marketing chief Robin L. Williams said Monday.

At the same time, former Meridian Bancorp officer Mark A. Turner has been named WSFS's managing vice president and controller.

At Meridian, Turner served most recently as controller of

Meridian Capital Markets, the company's investment arm.

A former senior manager at the Philadelphia office of accounting firm KPMG Peat Marwick, Turner also helped manage mergers and acquisitions for Meridian, which bought other banks at a rate of more than one a year, before it was itself acquired by CoreStates Financial Corp. earlier this year.

But marketing chief Williams said Turner's "overall strength as a controller" — not his expertise in mergers — was the main factor in his hiring. "We recruited him hard," Williams said.

Turner will succeed former WSFS controller Jerry Holbrook, who quit in March to join First USA Bank, the Wilmington-based credit card giant.

WSFS is also interviewing candidates for chief lending officer, who will supervise a staff of more than 60 credit officers and support staff.

The executives now being replaced left last winter following the end of a seven-month effort by the bank's board of directors to find a buyer willing to pay a premium for the $1.5 billion-asset company.

The effort was abandoned when Reading, Pa.-based Sovereign Bancorp and other would-be suitors declined to pay much more than the approximately $9 a share at which WSFS stock was then trading. The stock has lately traded at above $10 a share, its highest level since 1989. It closed Monday at $9.875.

The Wilmington News Journal announces
Mark's hiring, alongside Tom Stevenson, 1996.

Auto leases hurt thrift

WSFS to take charge of $3.4 million to cover the portfolio's losses

By JONATHAN D. EPSTEIN
Staff reporter

WSFS Financial Corp. on Tuesday said it expects to take a second-quarter charge of about $3.4 million before taxes, or about 24 cents per share, to cover anticipated losses on its auto lease portfolio.

The Wilmington-based thrift said it would take the charge on its $216 million used car lease portfolio because of the declining value of used vehicles.

The charge, which equals about $2.5 million after taxes, is about 60 percent of WSFS' first-quarter earnings of $4.2 million.

WSFS' various business ventures were reported
in the Wilmington News Journal.

WSFS' online bank is sold

Everbank hasn't turned a profit

By JONATHAN D. EPSTEIN
Staff reporter

WSFS Financial Corp. has agreed to sell its Everbank.com subsidiary to a Florida financial services investment firm, ending the Wilmington-based company's venture into Internet-only banking as it refocuses on its Delaware roots.

Alliance Capital Partners Inc., of Jacksonville, is paying an undisclosed price to buy St. Louis-based CustomerOne Financial Network Inc., which operates Everbank. WSFS would get a "modest dollar premium" over its net investment in Everbank, which fell from $5.5 million to $2.3 million in value as of March 31.

Everbank has just over $300 million in deposits and $28 million in loans. The sale is expected to close at the end of the third quarter or beginning of the fourth, pending approval by regulators.

WSFS had announced plans in late April to sell Everbank as part of the thrift's efforts to streamline its operations and exit businesses that weren't profitable enough or part of its primary banking business in Delaware. Everbank, which was established in the fourth quarter of 1999, has yet to report a profit and its customer base is nationwide, not local.

Wilmington News Journal reports on WSFS selling Everbank, 2003.

WSFS thins out business

Reverse-mortgage portfolio is sold

By JONATHAN D. EPSTEIN
Staff reporter

WSFS Financial Corp., in another move to slim down and refocus on local banking, said Monday it has sold most of its reverse-mortgage portfolio to a Delaware affiliate of New York investment banking house Lehman Brothers Holdings Inc. for more than four times the portfolio's value.

The sale of WSFS' reverse mortgages to Lehman Brothers Bank ends a nine-year venture into a business that WSFS acquired but didn't build. The sale is the Wilmington-based thrift's fifth transaction since deciding last year to shed business lines that weren't central to the bank's deposit-taking and lending in Delaware.

"For the last two years, we've been on a strategic mission to focus on the core bank. Our focus going forward is on building our franchise in Delaware," said Mark Turner, WSFS chief financial officer and chief operating officer.

> Reverse mortgages are available to people 62 and older who have equity in their homes.

Reverse mortgages, which are available to people 62 and older with equity in their homes, are similar to regular mortgages except the bank pays the borrower, not the reverse, and the lender's equity – not the borrower's – grows.

Lehman Brothers, which first approached WSFS about a transaction in the spring, combined the WSFS loans with those of another Lehman subsidiary, Financial Freedom, and sold the combined portfolio to investors. WSFS will be paid a fee to continue servicing the loans under an agreement with Financial Freedom. The thrift still owns portions of other reverse mortgages that it continues to service for other lenders.

WSFS said it expects to receive net proceeds of $136 million in mostly cash from Lehman, the nation's fourth-largest brokerage firm by capital and a leader in bond trading and mortgage finance. The price is more than four times the portfolio's value of $33 million, resulting in a gain before taxes of $103 million and an after-tax gain for the fourth quarter of $67 million, or $7.02 per share.

The Wilmington News Journal reports on WSFS Reverse Mortgages, 2003.

Mark, Katie, Regina and Becky in Aspen, 2006.

Joan Sullivan displaying WSFS' new brand, circa 2004.

Karl Johnston in a Wilmington
News Journal ad from Sept. 2005.

WSFS Bank slated to open Camden office

By Bonnie Benton
Staff writer

WSFS Bank's newest venture in the Kent County banking industry began with a July 1 groundbreaking ceremony at the Camden Town Center on Route 13, Camden.

"We see Camden as an exciting growth opportunity," said Marvin "Skip" Schoenhals, WSFS Bank chairman and president. "The growth in the residential population – both occurring and planned – and the growth in small businesses already and density of small businesses in that area are very attractive to us."

No stranger to Kent County, the bank already has two operations in Dover – an in-store banking office located in the Metro Food Market and a loan center office on White Oak Road.

Schoenhals also said WSFS Bank also plans to open an office in west Dover on Route 8 in early 2005.

Expected to open in fall 2004, the Camden office will follow the bank's new prototype design – a design that was used at the Bear and Rehoboth locations.

The Camden location will offer all the bank's regular services, including checking and savings accounts, loans, mortgages, credit cards, CDs and small business services.

The location will employ about nine associates. The expected hours of operation will be from 9 a.m. to 6 p.m. Monday through Thursday, 9 a.m. to 7 p.m. Friday and 9 a.m. to 3 p.m. Saturday. The drive through window will be open from noon to 3 p.m. Sunday.

For more information, visit www.wsfsbank.com.

READY ...SET ...DIG! Karl Johnson, chief operating officer, Marvin "Skip" Schoenhals, chairman and president, and Mark Turner, chief operating officer, are pictured left to right turning the first soil at the site of WSFS Bank's new branch office in Camden. Photo courtesy of WSFS Bank.

Karl, Skip and Mark break ground on
a new branch in Camden, 2004.

WSFS will refund inappropriately charged fees

ATM glitch misinformed customers about balances

By JONATHAN D. EPSTEIN
Staff reporter

A snafu with WSFS Financial Corp.'s ATMs last month caused customers to accumulate hundreds of dollars in improper "not sufficient funds" fees because their receipts showed money available though deposits hadn't yet cleared.

WSFS officials said they are correcting the problem and will refund the NSF fees paid by any customer who was inappropriately charged. The Wilmington-based thrift, which has 55,000 customers in Delaware and surrounding areas, also said it was suspending a policy change that had led to the problem when it was instituted in early May.

Officials said fewer than 1 percent of the bank's customers were affected.

"We don't like to make mistakes, but we believe this affected a small number of our customers for only a short period of time," said Chief Operating Officer Mark Turner. "When we do make mistakes, we do right by our customers and we're in the process of doing that."

WSFS has long had a policy of paying checks written by customers in good standing even if they don't have the money in their account. The thrift charges the customer an NSF fee of $28.50, which is the same as the returned check fee, but officials say the policy saves customers embarrassment and credit problems from a check bouncing.

The recent problems stemmed from a May 8 decision to extend the policy to ATM withdrawals and point-of-sale purchases for up to $250, company officials said. At the same time, a glitch in the ATM system had machines confusing a customer's total balance – including deposits that hadn't cleared – with the available balance, so that ATM receipts reflected money that wasn't there.

Officials didn't realize there was a problem with their systems until complaints began mounting in late May.

John McKinny of Claymont had $65 in his account when he deposited a disability check on May 31 for $1,371.90 for his wife. Two days later, the 59-year-old customer went to a WSFS ATM to take out $110 in preparation for a trip to Atlantic City. The machine allowed a balance of more than $1,200. He then used his debit card to make two other purchases.

A few days later, McKinny said, he received a notice in the mail saying that he had been assessed $114 in fees for overdrawing his account.

Reach Jonathan D. Epstein at 324-2680 or jepstein@delawareonline.com.

The Wilmington News Journal reports on
WSFS refunding inappropriately charged fees, 2003.

A WSFS branch prototype.

The WSFS Headquarters at 838 N. Market Street in Wilmington,
which housed the bank from 1887-2007.

DRAFT

Mission (Purpose):

We Stand For Service™ and strengthening our communities.

Vision (View of the Future):

We envision a day when all our constituents say, "I can't imagine a world without WSFS."

Strategy (Business Model):

Engaged Associates delivering Stellar Service to create Customer Advocates, resulting in a high performing company.

Values (Culture and Behaviors):

- Committed to always doing the right thing
- Empowered to serve our Customers and community
- Dedicated to openness and candor
- Driven to grow and improve

An early version of WSFS' Mission, Vision
and Values from 2002–2003.

Mark, Skip and others celebrate the 175th anniversary
of WSFS by ringing the bell at the NASDAQ in 2007.

The WSFS Bank Center at 500 Delaware Avenue
in Wilmington, 2007–present.

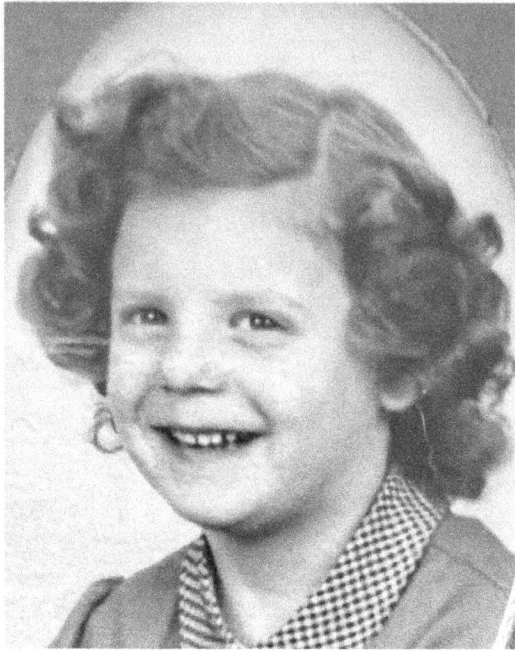

Peggy's Kindergarten photo.

The full Executive Team, 2012.

Peggy in front of the Bank Center, 2010.

The WSFS Culture Book
from 2017.

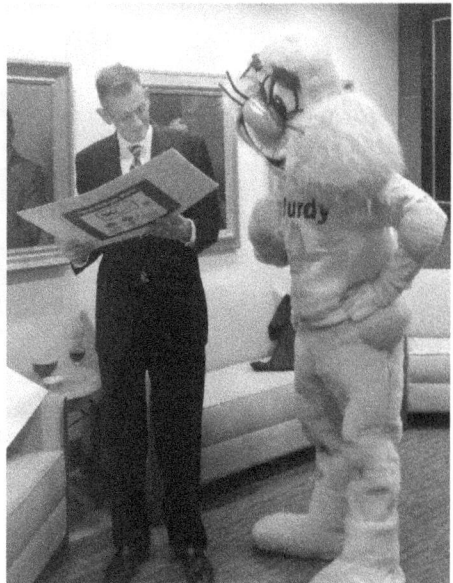

Mark and Jurdy.

Crisis: Treasury buys bank shares to spur lending

FROM PAGE A1

The Wilmington News Journal reports on the Financial Crisis.

Fed Funds Target

Fed Rate Hikes 2004-2006:
The Housing Market Boom

Fed Rate Cuts 2007-2008:
The Housing Market Crash

2008 Fed Rate Cuts:
The Great Recession

8.00%
7.00%
6.00%
5.00%
4.00%
3.00%
2.00%
1.00%
0.00%

Dec-03 Jun-04 Dec-04 Jun-05 Dec-05 Jun-06 Dec-06 Jun-07 Dec-07 Jun-08 Dec-08 Jun-09 Dec-09 Jun-10 Dec-10

The Federal Funds Rate in the years around the Financial Crisis.

TARP: Local stalwarts WSFS, Wilmington Trust confident

FROM PAGE F1

least 2011, according to a recent study by Bloomberg News.

"Somebody that has a lot of CRE exposure is going to be held to a higher standard" to redeem TARP preferred shares, said Paul Miller, a former bank examiner and now an analyst with FBR Capital Markets in Arlington, Va. "You've got to be careful they don't allow these guys to buy back TARP, and then a year goes by and have to give it back to them."

Among 35 of the biggest regional lenders that retain TARP funds, commercial real estate and construction loans average 37 percent of total loans, compared with 8.5 percent of Citigroup Inc. and Wells Fargo & Co., the two biggest U.S. banks that haven't announced plans to repay the government, according to data compiled by Bloomberg.

Wilmington Trust's commercial real estate and construction loans are 22 percent of the total. At WSFS, it's 9 percent.

"That's pretty big exposure," Andrew Stapp, an analyst who covers both banks for B. Riley & Company, said of Wilmington Trust. "Most banks are half that or less. That's where the bulk of their asset quality issues come from."

While acknowledging troubles in those portfolios, WSFS and Wilmington Trust – which actually received the money through an effort similar to TARP called the Capital Purchase Program, or CPP – don't believe it's enough to put payback at risk.

"Why are we different? We are not in those kinds of markets," Ted T. Cecala, Wilmington Trust's chairman and CEO, said of the booming development days in such cities as Las Vegas and Miami. "No. 2, we do not lend to high-rise office buildings or mega-malls. Our exposure would be to owner-occupied properties ... Or it would be to people who have developed a strip mall or a medical office building, something that's fairly low-risk."

At WSFS, there's been a deliberate effort for some years now to keep residential construction loans – where many of the delinquency problems lie – relatively small. The average commercial real estate loan is for about $1.3 million, for a small strip shopping center in an established area, and only when the loan-to-value ratio is low, said Mark A. Turner, president and CEO.

"Locally and for WSFS, there is much less concern," about "CRE," or commercial real estate loans, Turner said. "That's because of the quality and the character of our commercial real estate loans. ... Do I think CRE's going to get in the way [of repayment]? Certainly not."

Stapp sees issues nonetheless with WSFS' condition.

"Their capital position is stronger, but [I] think there's still concerns with WSFS, primarily in its construction and development portfolio," he said. "The charge-offs in that portfolio have been much higher than Wilmington Trust."

Commercial real estate troubles do have to be a key consideration in the timing of the payback, executives said. And analysts say that lingering problems with loan quality, and thus earnings, could mean that banks would have to accomplish a payback using other sources of money - sources that aren't necessarily the best for business at this time.

Analysts generally would like to see banks keep capital ratios strong with the help of CPP money, then be sure the economy has turned around before they consider paying it back, said Avi Barak, an analyst who covers WSFS for Sandler O'Neill & Partners.

Analysts are most cautious over the possibility that the banks will have to resort to a sale of more shares to raise the

Mark Turner, president and CEO of WSFS Bank, doesn't think commercial real estate loan troubles will stand in the way of repaying TARP money.

News Journal file/WILLIAM BRETZGER

HOW'S THEIR YEAR?

WSFS Bank

Treasury funds received:
$52.6 million

Share performance:
52-week change: -42.62 percent
52-week high (Jan. 6): $49.50
52-week low (March 5): $16.47

Wilmington Trust

Treasury funds received:
$330 million

Share performance:
52-week change: -49.20 percent
52-week high
(Dec. 10, 2008): $24.10
52-Week low (March 6): $6.79

Sources: Yahoo Finance, FDIC

cash, a move that banks don't want to make at a time when both Wilmington Trust and WSFS share prices are off more than 40 percent from a year ago, leading many more shares of common stock now would in effect "dilute" the value of other investors' existing shares, and dim the banks' market appeal.

"I don't think it would sit well with the investment community for them to pay TARP and not do some type of capital raise," Stapp said of Wilmington Trust.

Lingering under government oversight too long also could create perception problems for a bank, analysts say, but bankers see a greater risk in being too soon. Local economic signals will be a prime timing consideration for local executives, who believe it's key to exit the program into a climate of gathering strength.

"You don't want to start this repayment process with unemployment continuing to rise" locally, Cecala said. His bank believes that the diverse business

model it has built – one that depends on a variety of fee-based businesses for revenue – will give it the liquidity and stability to pay back the government.

Banks also have to be careful they do not deplete their cushion of capital too much with a payback. Both banks are considered "well-capitalized" by regulators even without the added cushion of CPP money. With the earnings boost an economic recovery might bring, the banks could avoid having to consider selling more stock, analysts said.

Both banks are also convinced that they ultimately need to be out of the program – especially in order to be able to thrive in a recovery.

"It did come with significant restrictions that, maybe now, but maybe when the economy recovers, could affect our business," Turner said. At WSFS, the levels of liquidity, earnings and capital are healthy enough that Turner says he'll be knocking on Treasury Secretary Timothy Geithner's door as soon as there are clear signs of sustained economic health on the local and national fronts.

In the meantime, the "cushion" of the CPP money is still helping the bank grow and thrive, he said. WSFS hired 30-40 net workers this year, and expects to do the same in 2010. Loan growth is on line for a 4 percent to 6 percent uptick this year.

"We're planning next year to grow again 4 to 6 percent," he said.

At Wilmington Trust, the future also seems far more positive than it has.

"Over the first five to 10 months this year, there's been an absence of the national builders [starting projects here]," Cecala said. "Now, we're starting to see them come into the market. Those are some of the signs you want to see."

Contact Jim Weiss at 324-2790 or jweiss@delawareonline.com.

Mark is featured in a Wilmington News Journal article about WSFS and TARP.

Mark and WSFS Associates in a 2009 Group Photo.

A ribbon cutting ceremony at the Kennett Square Branch in PA
around 2010. Left to right is Rick Wright, Shari Kruzinski,
Mark Turner and Gail Chase, branch manager.

Project

GREAT

Growing Relationships & Engaging Associates Together

So what's the buzz about **GREAT**? What is everybody talking about anyway? Here are some answers to the questions that may be swirling around in your head.

What is GREAT? Coined by Lauren Kubler, it stands for *Growing Relationships and Engaging Associates Together.*

Project *GREAT* is a bankwide initiative, focused on growing our brand and capturing market share during this period of merger and disruption among our competitors. In a sense, it is an acquisition without the red tape!

Who? You and the entire WSFS family. This includes our WSFS advocates; our Board of Directors and Advisory Boards, as well as Customers. Really anybody who wants to introduce their friends to our Bank.

When? The time is now! Several internal *GREAT* Teams have been identified to lead the effort to gain market share. All Associates will be participating in the success of this project. We need everyone's support and yes, there will be prizes!!

Why? Are you kidding me?? WSFS will soon be the oldest and largest independent bank and trust company in Delaware. We have strengthened our community and serviced our customers for almost 179 years. While other

The Message of Project GREAT, 2010.

Ted Weschler has dinner with Warren Buffett for the first time
in July 2010, and they show their support for WSFS.

A View from
the Boardroom—Volume III

As a result of our longer-term orientation and our commitment to being high performing, we believe investors in WSFS should be those with a long-term, high performance orientation as well.

Marvin N. Schoenhals and Charles G. Cheleden

Dear Fellow Shareholders:

In keeping with the practice we began two years ago, we are pleased to provide our third perspective on selected thoughts of interest to the Owners of WSFS. We continue to view this letter as a companion piece to management's letter on the preceding pages. These letters recognize the partnership between an effective board and an effective management team that is critical to a successful company.

Our goal in these boardroom letters is to share the board's key philosophies that guide our oversight of the Company. Space limitations make it impossible to review all of those thoughts each year. Thus, to get a more complete picture, we urge Shareholders to read the previous letters, as well as our Board Principles and Guidelines document. They can be found at investors.wsfsbank.com.

The main subject of our first letter in the 2012 Report was about the process we had begun of "board renewal." We started that process in 2011. At that point we had 15 directors with an average age of 61. Today we have 10 with an average age of 56. More significantly, three new directors, with an average age of 49 have joined the board. The impact of this reduction in size and "new blood" has been significant. Discussions are more strategic, focused, engaged and with a sharing of perspectives where seasoned, intermediate and newer directors are learning and advancing together. While we will continue to actively manage the board, no changes are being proposed for this year. We would also like you to know that as part of the process of constantly seeking to improve our performance, we periodically perform an assessment of the performance of the board, evaluating ourselves collectively and the quality of individuals'

contributions. In most years we do this through a self-directed process. However, in early 2015 we utilized the resources of an outside firm to enhance the process.

In our 2013 letter we emphasized the commitment to being a high-performing Company. We explained how we hold ourselves accountable to that goal by asking: "Are we creating Total Shareholder Return (TSR) relative to our peers?" More pointedly, we must continually earn the right to remain independent. We explained that our goal is to behave as long-term Owners, which means we compare TSR over three, five, seven and 10 year time frames. The letter last year has significant detail on the mechanics of our calculations that result in 160 data points of comparison to our peers regarding TSR. That letter also explained that we cannot control how the market values WSFS at any point in time; however, if we maintain high performance metrics, appropriate valuations will follow. The expectations we have are to be in the top quintile of results of similar banking organizations for a combination of: Return on Assets (ROA), Return on Equity (ROE), and Growth in Earnings Per Share (GEPS). Our pledge is to report this data each year in this report (more later).

We want to share again a thought that we mention whenever we talk to investors about WSFS:

As a result of our longer-term orientation and our commitment to being high performing, we believe investors in WSFS should be those with a long-term, high performance orientation as well.

It is this long-term view, coupled with a highly disciplined focus on performance, that leads us to maintain a "classified" or "staggered" board structure. As a result, approximately one-third

One of the bank's "From the Boardroom" letters.

WSFS Financial Corporation

Financial Highlights

(Dollars in millions)

at December 31,	2012	2011	2010
Total assets	$ 4,375	$ 4,289	$ 3,954
Net loans, including held for sale	$ 2,737	$ 2,713	$ 2,576
Mortgage-backed securities and other investments	$ 952	$ 908	$ 803
Deposits	$ 3,275	$ 3,135	$ 2,811
Borrowings	$ 637	$ 724	$ 748
Stockholders' equity	$ 421	$ 392	$ 368
Number of full-service branches	41	40	36

(Dollars in thousands, except earnings per share data)

for the years ended December 31,	2012	2011	2010
Net income	$31,311	$ 22,677	$ 14,117
Net income allocable to common stockholders	$28,541	$ 19,907	$ 11,347
Diluted earnings per common share	$ 3.25	$ 2.28	$ 1.46
Return on average assets	0.73 %	0.56 %	0.37%
Return on tangible common equity	9.15 %	7.03 %	4.35%
Nonperforming assets to total assets	1.43 %	2.14 %	2.35%

Mission
We Stand For Service®

Vision
We envision a day when all our constituents say, "I can't imagine a world without WSFS."

Strategy
Engaged Associates delivering Stellar Service growing Customer Advocates and value for our Owners.℠

Values
At WSFS we:
- Do the right thing
- Serve others
- Are open and candid
- Grow and improve

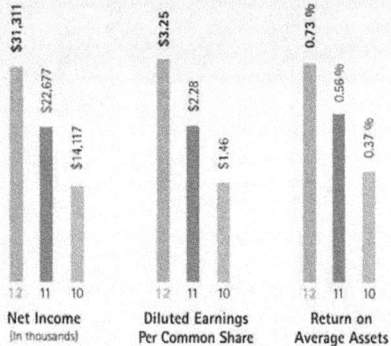

Net Income (In thousands)
- $31,311 (12)
- $22,677 (11)
- $14,117 (10)

Diluted Earnings Per Common Share
- $3.25 (12)
- $2.28 (11)
- $1.46 (10)

Return on Average Assets
- 0.73 % (12)
- 0.56 % (11)
- 0.37 % (10)

Part of WSFS' 2012 Annual Report.

Financial
Highlights

(Dollars in millions)

At December 31,	2014	2013	2012
Total assets	$ 4,853	$ 4,516	$ 4,375
Net loans, including held for sale	$ 3,185	$ 2,936	$ 2,737
Mortgage-backed securities and other investments	$ 919	$ 890	$ 952
Deposits	$ 3,649	$ 3,187	$ 3,275
Borrowings	$ 668	$ 904	$ 637
Stockholders' equity	$ 489	$ 383	$ 421
Number of offices	55	52	52
Number of full-service retail branches	43	39	41

(Dollars in thousands, except earnings per share data)

For the years ended December 31,	2014	2013	2012
Net income	$53,757	$46,882	$31,311
Diluted earnings per common share	$ 5.78	$ 5.06	$ 3.25
Return on average assets	1.17%	1.07%	0.73%
Return on tangible common equity	13.80%	13.60%	9.15%
Nonperforming assets to total assets	1.08%	1.06%	1.43%

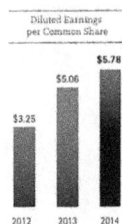

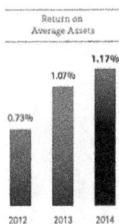

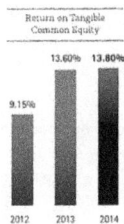

Diluted Earnings per Common Share	Return on Average Assets	Return on Tangible Common Equity
2012: $3.25	2012: 0.73%	2012: 9.15%
2013: $5.06	2013: 1.07%	2013: 13.60%
2014: $5.78	2014: 1.17%	2014: 13.80%

WSFS' 2014 Financial Highlights.

A wall at WSFS' HQ showing the company's history
of acquisitions and brands.

WSFS' 2018 Annual Report.

Mark on the cover of American Banker in 2018.

Rodger Levenson. CEO 2019–present.

Leadership, Service...and Silver Linings

Congratulations to Mark Turner for his 25+ years of service to WSFS Bank.

As a friend and colleague, it's challenging to put into words the gratitude we feel for someone who has had such a tremendous impact on WSFS.

It was during Mark's tenure as CEO & President that *We Stand For Service* became our brand and our mission. He embraced the challenges of the Great Recession and turned them into silver linings. Mark led WSFS through an era of unprecedented growth, and he was instrumental as we expanded our wealth business and deepened our roots in Southeastern Pennsylvania.

The WSFS sign, now a part of the Philadelphia skyline, is our beacon to serve and stands as a testament to his lasting contributions.

Mark's journey will be memorialized in WSFS history. He enriched our Culture, transformed our Company and strengthened our Community. That is his enduring legacy, and we are forever grateful.

On behalf of all of us at WSFS, I wish Mark the best as he begins his next chapter.

Rodger Levenson
Chairman, President and CEO
WSFS Bank

WSFS bank
We Stand For Service

WSFS congratulating Mark on his retirement
in the American Banker, 2022.

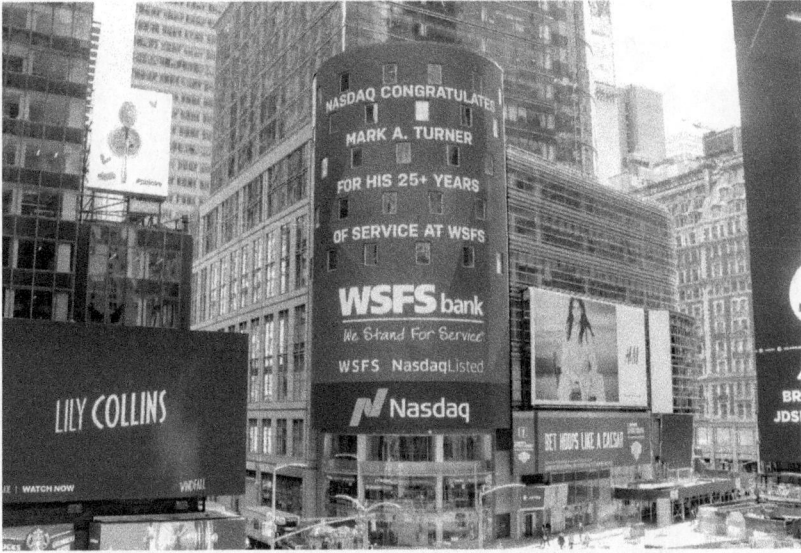

Mark and WSFS featured on the NASDAQ in Times Square.

Rodger, Skip and Mark: three generations of CEO.

Mark with Skip at the opening of the MAT Center,
in the WSFS Philly headquarters, 2022.

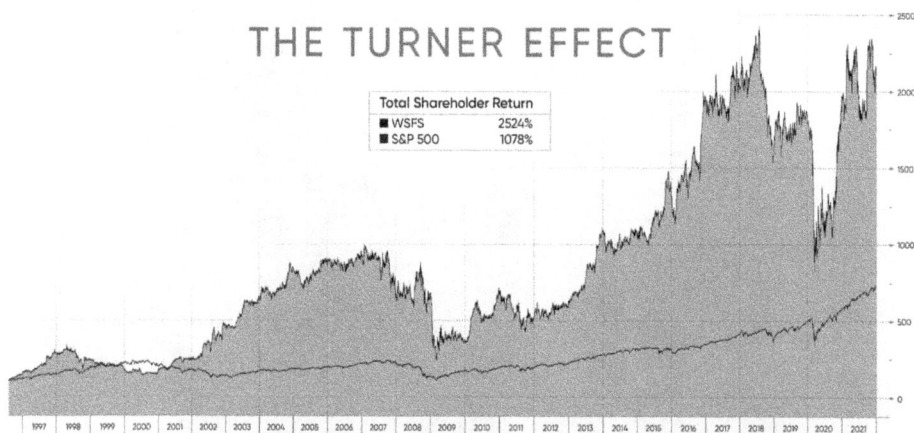

THE TURNER EFFECT

Total Shareholder Return	
■ WSFS	2524%
■ S&P 500	1078%

WSFS' shareholder return performance
over Mark's tenure vs. the S&P 500.

The Turners, 2023.

Mark's portrait at WSFS headquarters.

WSFS' Main Office at 500 Delaware Avenue, 2007–present.

WSFS' Market Street headquarters in the
Philadelphia skyline, 2019–present.

THIRTEEN | BIG CHANGES IN THE BOARDROOM

By Mark Turner

B y 2012, the crisis and recession were mostly over, and the typical "creative destruction" opportunities were plentiful in the marketplace. Everything from key talent and teams to new products and services, to technologies and whole businesses were available, and at generationally good prices. Much of the bank's leadership yearned to pursue these, especially while many of our competitors were paralyzed by deep problems or uncertainty. We had a bold vision of pulling two strategic plan cycles of investments into one. The time had come for more aggressive, calculated risk-taking—an imperative for catapulting us into a new level of success.

Historically, bank board members were picked by the CEO, and had enjoyed compensated, near-lifetime appointments, akin to justices on the Supreme Court. The WSFS board had grown to 15 members, through good intent but lack of care, like an unpruned hedgerow. Many of the members had guided the institution through its most trying times, safeguarding the bank's future. Yet, as I surveyed the evolving landscape, it became increasingly apparent that many WSFS board members were scarred—not ready to embrace the rich opportunities the market presented.

As Ted noted in his reflections, a chasm had opened between management and the board, with those steeped in a conservative ethos inadvertently stifling the innovation and growth opportunities. The boardroom conversations, once vibrant and strategic, had devolved into exercises in box-checking, driven by fear rather than a shared vision for progress. As Skip reflected later, *The board had become too large, cumbersome, too many voices, too risk averse; bogged down in detail and individual strong opinions.*

During a prior board retreat in nearby Baltimore, set against the backdrop of the financial crisis, I had watched how the board members handled pressure—some froze like deer in headlights; while others rolled up their sleeves, determined to forge ahead. It struck me that, as crucial as a single leader might be in a crisis or an opportunity, it's the team huddled in that metaphorical foxhole, shoulder to shoulder, that can make or break that leader's ability to have impact. And here lay the crux of my challenge: The board, as my direct overseers, wielded substantial influence over our next steps. The time for change had come.

We found ourselves grappling with the dilemma of how to transform our governance. Could we really ask long-time board members, who had highly influential standing in the community and were passionate about WSFS, to step aside? Yet, how could WSFS truly flourish if the board dynamic we had was an impediment to our growth?

After extensive discussions, a few of us approached the full board with a proposition to reduce the board's size from 15 to 10. We told them that the board was too big, the composition was off, the thinking too conservative for our strategy. At WSFS, we had been nimble; we had been calculated risk-takers adjusting quickly to optimize situations. These were the strategic advantages we had. To keep any competitive edge, we had to pursue opportunities with a faster, more aggressive, more united approach.

That sentiment resonated and became unanimous in the boardroom: that a smaller, more dynamic board was critical to seizing the post-crisis market circumstances before they slipped away. However, the path forward remained fraught with challenges. The governance committee, composed of seven of our most seasoned members, was stymied by how to implement the change. Confronted with the reality that their peers, friends, or they themselves could potentially be ousted, the committee's deliberations became overrun by emotion.

The difficulty of dismantling these long-held relationships made it clear that our governance committee would also not be able to propose the needed changes. So, the board whittled the committee down further, to a group of four—Skip, CG, Ted, and me—to achieve our downsizing goals.

Telling successful people that they needed to step aside for the organization's greater good was no small challenge. Some of them took it as if they were being fired—and most had never been fired from anything in their lives. I can remember clearly how intensely I felt the burden. I had good relationships with these people. Two board members had made me a trustee on their estates (as I learned later, that is *not* a good idea). Another board member's spouse called me saying how much angst this person was in, and to please handle it gently. It was a long, hard road, and we frequently had to remind members that we all needed to do what was best for the company.

Gradually, the dialogue bore fruit. A highly respected member,

Tom Preston, volunteered to step down, acknowledging that he had served for many years and there was a need for new perspectives. This professional, selfless move allowed others to step down more gracefully. A few resisted, fearing it was too much change, reluctant to relinquish their positions. The thorny, arduous process spanned *over two years*.

By 2014, we were slimmed down to a board of ten—much smaller, and just as importantly, with several new members. We also had a new board "social contract": We now stressed that each seat was extremely valuable. If someone wasn't substantially contributing, even if they were fully engaged, or if we needed their seat for someone with different expertise, they could be asked to step aside in due course. And it was to be an ongoing process. Like any senior leader, you had to earn your right to be on the board every year. Like Skip, lead director CG Cheleden was one of my partners in this board reconstruction period, and we worked to create a system to refresh the board routinely so we did not get stale. "If there was a weak link, or somebody wanted out, we needed to know and act," CG recalls.

We also proposed an ideal "tenure diversity" that would guide the optimal mix and refreshment: A third of board members should be in their first five years of tenure, a third should have served between five and 10 years, and a third should have more than 10 years of service. Around 15 years would be the upper limit. This structure kept refreshment active, and balanced younger members with new ideas and energy, with seasoned members who boasted more experience and institutional knowledge.

Further, every three years, we had a multi-day board retreat to discuss the upcoming strategic cycle, and what direction we wanted to go in. Then we would take those ideas and develop the three-year plan—distributing it throughout the company so that everyone knew what we were up to. "It was a great unifier for everybody, no one was out in the cold," CG said.

Importantly, around that time we would also explore if we had the right board composition to be successful for the next generation of the strategic plan. This helped instill the necessity that the board composition had to align strongly with the needs of the company—not for the past, but for our future.

Another initiative Skip and CG implemented to help stress the board's important role and accountability was our "From the Boardroom" letter. Instead of having just one message from management in our annual report to shareholders, there was also a letter from the board, demonstrating how our collective leadership was united, yet we all understood our different roles. It became a way to share the board's culture, philosophies, and scorecards for success with our owners. Out of this, the board's "Principles and Guidelines" were developed and publicly posted on our website.

One of the most important things I recognized throughout this period is that it's crucial to make sure you don't have a board that is much stronger than your management team, or a management team that's much stronger than your board. They each need to be strong, have more or less equal horsepower, and be continually raising the bar on each other. While board members are a CEO's bosses, they are also partners. I was blessed to have wise partners, and newer board members, like Cal Morgan, Anat Bird, and J.J. Davis (as well as the longer-tenured members, Skip, CG, and Ted) as trusted advisors, supporters, and constructive critics during this period. They made me a better CEO.

Principles for a Successful Board

1. Recognize that, with management, the board is the organization's most important team.
Board members select, motivate, and hold the CEO accountable to execute the mission and strategy according to the organization's values. The board also sets the tone of "Do/Do Not" within the organization—helping put the guardrails in for growth, innovation, and risk-taking.

2. Get to the right number.
The most effective and most efficient boards generally have 8–12 people. These are also the ones members feel provide the best experience and most fulfillment. The board should be as small as possible to get all the work done, with the right balance of expert and diverse voices. No one hides, everyone contributes. This enables strong, nimble, united decision-making.

3. Get to the right composition.
Match members' expertise to the strategic plan. Make sure there is a diversity of skills, experience, backgrounds, and constituent representation. Adhere to the tenure rule of thirds: approximately one-third of members with 1–5 years on the board, one-third with 5–10 years, and another third with 10–15 years. Be careful not to have too many retirees, lawyers, "celebrities," or ex-CEOs.

4. Create a good social contract—and continually self-police.
Stress that this is a serious job. Every seat is valuable. Board members are not members for life. At the table, members should be prepared to contribute; they should be collegial, constructive, and speak and vote with their conscience. There is no need for term limits or age limits, as members must continually earn their seat.

5. Partner with management.
Boards are at risk of having a strength and power imbalance with management. The goal should be to have each entity equally strong, and continually pushing each other to be better. Executive sessions of the board should be regular but restrained—avoid having two meetings where the agenda meeting is followed by the "real meeting" in an executive session. All meaningful discussions should take place in the boardroom, and with management present if at all possible; resist heavy sidebars and member cliques.

6. There should be a strong chair (and committee chairs).
The chairs should set the tone of board members working with each other and with management, ensuring that the board stays in the governance lane. They should work with the CEO to set the agenda; they should guide discussions; regulate the over-voiced and encourage the under-voiced members; and bring items to a quick, clear conclusion—or table items for later discussion. After appropriate analysis and discussion, they should seek decisions with buy-in, not necessarily unanimity. They should plan for crises and outside pressures, and set the tone for how to handle them.

7. Create an environment of constructive challenge and teamwork.
Board members should both support and challenge management as the situation merits—asking questions until they're satisfied. Big items should be reviewed at least twice before everyone votes. Stress that it's OK to vote "no," but no one should abstain (except in cases of conflict of interest). Dinners and off-sites are necessary for relationship building and group bonding.

8. Maximize focus on the strategic; relegate the tactical.
All heavy lifting should be done within the committees and presented to the full board to discuss and approve. Committee chairs should report out big items discussed to the full board at the following meeting. Short meeting pre-calls are helpful to prioritize topics and time, and to ensure that the materials needed to make an informed decision are present. Make generous use of a consent agenda for routine and administrative matters.

9. Plan for crisis and dilemmas.
Tough moments will arise. Have a small, board "crisis team" ready with access to expert resources, both internal and external. Routinely "scenario plan" for problems. When a dilemma arises, ask the following three questions, in this order: 1) What is the right thing to do in accordance with our mission and values? 2) How can we create value out of this situation, regardless? 3) If a decision does not comport with public, press, or political sentiment, how do we explain it well and then stand by it?

10. Set processes for board self-improvement and refreshment. Implement post-meeting surveys with short, simple, questions which must be answered in a timely manner. There should be annual board self-assessments and gap analysis, with an outside expert/facilitator to help every three years. Comments should be synthesized, constructive, and not attributed to any one person. Curate an active pipeline and succession plan for the board as members are nearing the end of their tenures. Train board leadership skills using committee chair roles.

FOURTEEN | THE CRUCIBLE

By Mark Turner

Apart from the start of our work transforming the board, the year 2012 was shaping up to be a watershed period for WSFS in many other respects. We were on a steady path back towards good profitability. We were working on the next turn—the post-crisis, growth turn—of our strategic plan. We had recruited a lot of new talent into our ranks, like former local banks CEOs Paul Geraghty and Donna Coughey. And we were picking up good market share from the recent bank implosions all around us.

But before the 2013–2015 plan could take flight, we had one huge obstacle standing in our way: our new regulator, the Office of the Comptroller of Currency (OCC), was putting us through our first critical examination.

No Roses Till it Closes

A regulatory examination is never a pleasant thing, but our first with the OCC started in 2011 and was especially vexing. The OCC was under intense political and public pressure for not having done their job before the crisis, and we came to be under them through legislative mandate when our former regulator, the Office of Thrift Supervision (OTS), was put out of existence by Dodd-Frank in 2010.

The OTS was widely thought to have been especially lax; responsible for the mortgage bubble getting out of hand and for some high-profile failures. Unfortunately for us, we were also under a regulatory enforcement action, an MOU, by the OTS. So, when the OCC took over, they assumed WSFS was not only a problem situation, but also one that had not been well regulated—and, given the pressure on them, the OCC was in no position or mood to give us the benefit of the doubt. Suffice it to say, in our first exam, they kicked the tires very hard.

As the exam progressed in the spring of 2012, we felt the steel-toed shoe. We came upon a substantial difference of opinion with the OCC regarding several large loans that we believed were "money good" in many cases—although the primary business may have had debt service or cash flow challenges from the recession, the sponsor had sufficient other cash flow or other collateral they could sell to ensure we'd be repaid in full, even if it was a bit of a twisting path to get there.

We'd had a good history with this. Our former regulator, the OTS, had allowed us to take this broader-picture view towards asset classification—meaning those loans could be classified as good loans. The OCC, however, made us adopt a whole new loan risk–rating system that was much more stringent, and would result in these loans being classified as problems. And with more loans marked as problems, we had to set aside more reserves, resulting in more losses and less capital.

Problem loans were particularly troublesome during this period, especially when you had too many. There were unspoken regulatory thresholds for the ratio of problem loans to capital that could land you in serious trouble. Moreover, these limits were both unclear and frequently shifting.

What *was* very clear in this environment, was that the regulator was always going to win any argument about problems loans. If our exam concluded, and our position worsened because of the exam, it was highly likely we would be subject to a new, harsher regulatory order. And if we just stayed our course, our position would definitely have worsened.

I was quite anxious. These outcomes would be public: damaging our reputation, which would be damning, as it would inhibit customer and associate recruiting and shake the market's confidence in us. A new regulatory action would also force us to focus internally for a long time to come, with little control of our destiny, and without being able to pursue growth and other opportunities until we straightened out our situation.

I knew that cleaning things up to a regulator's satisfaction could take a while. Even after we took pains to make the fixes they asked for, they said we had to demonstrate "sustained performance" with no guidance on how long we'd have to wait. (As I sit here today, in late 2024, Wells Fargo is still under restrictions on their growth from their 2018 regulatory order.) These possibilities threatened to put a damper on all the other watershed initiatives we had going for us.

Against this backdrop, the second quarter of 2012 would be a crucial crucible test for the bank, and for me. With more loans marked as problems under new OCC guidance, and the attendant large losses that came with those marks, we were up against the wall. A harsher regulatory response and its harmful consequences loomed. I knew we had to end the quarter in better shape than we began.

So, we put in place a new plan, dubbed our "Asset Strategies" program, and set up two war rooms. In one, Rodger managed the bad assets we could sell in short order at a loss, but still at decent prices, to relieve our problem asset pressure. In the other, the treasury team and I worked on the good, non-core assets we had in the business that we could sell to quickly generate gains that would offset those losses. Alongside these efforts, the commercial team worked with a list of solid, but temporarily delinquent customers to bring their loans current; and our asset liability committee repositioned our investments and borrowings for better future profitability. It was a daily battle on several fronts. And in financial markets that were still queasy, the possibilities were constantly changing.

As a result of prior, good risk-taking we had some especially valuable assets we could liquidate quickly. Earlier in the cycle, we had bought some mortgage-backed securities from vehicles that had blown up in the crisis. They were repackaged by investment banks to now be very solid investments (called resecuritization of real-estate mortgage investment conduits, or Re-REMICs). But given their tainted past, we were able to buy them at exceptionally good prices relative to their ultimate value. As the climate got better and the securities performed, these assets climbed dramatically in value, even above what we thought they were worth. These investments—savvily pursued by Ron Samuels and Paul Greenplate in treasury, and approved by the board after lengthy analyses and discussions—were a saving grace.

The war rooms worked long hours at a fevered pace. There were sleepless nights for sure. Each day we had to adjust what we could sell, and what price we could get for assets, both good and bad, pulling the trigger when things looked optimal. While Ron Samuels worked the markets for the best price for our good assets, Andrew Tauber led the daily slog to find a market for our problem loans and repossessed assets. There were ups and downs, and I would pop my head in almost every day to see how things were going. Andrew was a master at finding the best execution for problems—through auctions, private entities, and all types of distressed asset buyers. When I would congratulate him after we signed a deal, he would respond with a disciplined, "No roses till it closes." He was right. For those assets in that market, it was never a done deal until the money was in the bank.

Through these intense efforts on the part of an amazing team of people, we did it. In July 2012, we reported our second quarter results: Instead of losses and worse problem assets, we tallied positive net income for the quarter, increased capital, a 30 percent reduction in problem assets and an over 50 percent improvement in delinquent loans. We also positioned the balance sheet for better earnings for the years to come. These results gave us, the board, the market, and critically, our new, skeptical regulator, the confidence that we were not only better than we had looked, but that we had the will and ability to deftly manage our problems and opportunities. Fittingly, and very gratefully, I sent a dozen roses to Andrew when that quarter ended.

It was because of those war room efforts that seminal quarter, and our trust-building with the OCC, that we were released from our years-old, constraining regulatory order in February 2013. We could now be off and running. This intense period also gave me increased confidence in Rodger's executive leadership and potential: he was calm and steady, he did what was best for the whole company, and he got things done while adhering to our values, even in the toughest moments.

A Big Bet on WSFS

As we worked on the 2013–2015 strategic plan, we were now much more confident that the vehicle was in good shape, and that we had both hands on the wheel. Over the previous five years, the team had struggled mightily, and worked incredibly hard to confront so many challenges while moving us forward. Financial rewards were few: we faithfully followed our compensation plans, which said that we wouldn't get bonuses if we didn't make money; and if we only made a little bit of money, we'd get little bonuses. As a result, that period brought years of either no bonuses or negligible ones. Pay-for-performance was an important part of our culture.

So, as we approached our new strategic plan period, the board asked me, *What will keep you and this talented team here and motivated?* I believed the company was well positioned. We had the strategy, culture, team, changing board dynamic, and marketplace environment to excel...if we executed. And I believed in our ability to execute.

I also knew I had set six more years on my personal leadership clock at WSFS, and I was going to run hard through the tape. So, I took a big bet on WSFS, the team, and myself. I asked that the team's incentives be skewed: less if we just did OK, more if we did really well. And I went all-in on my incentives. I asked that options on shares of the company that I might earn for the next five years be replaced by an equal-value, one-time grant of options given to me right then. These options had our normal restrictions and vesting provisions, and importantly, their strike price was 20 percent out of the money, meaning the company's share value would have to increase by at least 20 percent for them to be worth anything.

In the board meeting to approve these plans, Skip reminded me that my five-year plan could be worth little to nothing if we didn't execute, the market didn't cooperate, or if many other things happened that were out of our control. Was I OK with that? The board would not replace or reprice those options. I said yes. That was what I wanted. I was confident in our strategy, culture, and team.

I then doubled down and asked that 40 percent of the options they would otherwise grant me be given to the team on the same terms, on top of their rebalanced plan. They deserved it. And I knew the team was key to our future success, my future success, and making these options (and the company) extremely valuable. By doing this, I felt I was only magnifying the possibility for positive results.

Part of our compensation culture at WSFS was that management should be highly incentivized to achieve real, long-term value creation. However, management should only get rewarded if the owners of the company were rewarded first, and by much more. The board unanimously approved these plans, and they were approved in a shareholder vote by 99 percent.

This was another watershed moment. Executive incentives were now fully aligned with our goal of sustained excellence through strategy, culture, and team.

FIFTEEN | GOOD TO GREAT

By Mark Turner

Ask anyone in the banking industry, and they'll tell you that the years directly following the 2008 crisis were the toughest ones for keeping up employee morale. From 2009 through 2012, our sector was rife with layoffs, austerity measures, mergers, failures, leadership shake-ups, and harsh regulatory actions. Those years were like trudging through mud and glass. And having disenchanted, anxious employees would not help recovery efforts.

At WSFS, we were determined to be different. We went above and beyond to make sure associates knew that we had their backs—leaning on our efforts with Gallup and our strong culture to keep spirits up. While other companies cut salaries, laid off personnel, limited extras like employee training, and implemented all kinds of restrictions; we continued to prioritize the physical, mental, and economic health of the people who were doing the hard work to pull the company through those dark days.

We kept annual pay raises, benefits, 401(k) matches, training, and development. But we also knew that small gestures mattered. I remember a particular moment that embodied our approach. Peggy came to me, mentioning that an associate had told her it was okay if we stopped having free coffee available in the office as a cost-saving measure. I loved the sentiment, but that outcome was ridiculous to me. "When the day comes that we can't afford a cup of coffee for our associates, we should shut our doors," I said. Peggy agreed, and that's how we proceeded—by maintaining the little things that made a big difference. I even upped the ante and suggested a coffee taste test, letting associates choose their favorite brew at their location. And we continued celebratory things like our ritual of cakes, balloons, and cards when associates had birthdays and work anniversaries.

The results of our big and small initiatives were well worth it. Through this difficult time, our Gallup associate-engagement scores were repeatedly over 10 times greater than the national average; our customer engagement was ranked as world-class; and we consistently received community support awards. The *Wilmington News Journal* named WSFS the number-one, best place to work in the local market for three years in a row.

Cultural cohesiveness was the organizational glue that held us together through a time that threatened to tear banks apart. Institutions that lacked this strong foundation often fractured beyond repair.

The World Turned Upside Down

During this period, it quickly became evident that the local landscape around us had changed. It was like a hurricane had blown through, leaving some houses standing and others severely damaged or gone. In particular, the sale of Wilmington Trust left a significant void in our region—one that M&T, although a very good bank, was ill-equipped to fill, because they were based in Buffalo, New York. Their out-of-market leadership understandably lacked the sensitivity needed for a community in transition, dismantling operations without a full appreciation of the ripple effects they would have in the area. It became clear to us that there was an opportunity to meet needs that remained unaddressed—a chance to uplift the local economy and strengthen our own business.

In early 2011, our executive team launched Project GREAT (Growing Relationships & Engaging Associates Together), an organization-wide commitment to better serve the community in ways that M&T could not. We engaged with disenfranchised Wilmington Trust bankers, strategically added branches and offices to enhance local accessibility, established a true wealth management unit, and amplified our business lending efforts to compensate for the diminished local competition. We were building and hiring at a time when others were still cutting or stagnant, and this certainly attracted positive attention.

One example that stands out to me is how we picked up talent during this ripe time, as with the hiring of Paul Geraghty. Paul was a local, exceptionally talented, well-respected executive banker, and a former CEO as well. His career had been sidetracked in the banking crisis, but he still had many years and lots to give. Rodger invited him to speak to us at an offsite about our GREAT efforts, and a relationship quickly grew. Soon I was speaking with him about our future, and I made the decision to hire him as our new head of wealth management. For the next decade, until his retirement, Paul led our wealth efforts. He cleaned up that nascent business, pulled parts together into a cohesive whole; grew the unit at a high and healthy rate, including through acquisitions; and ultimately made the division much more profitable and reputable. He was a wise, collaborative voice on our executive team during the difficult post-crisis time, and then in a rapid growth period. He also acted as a coach for Rodger as he was growing into his eventual role as CEO of WSFS. Paul's contributions to WSFS were immeasurable.

Meanwhile, around this time, we applied to join the US government's next turn in rehabilitating the economy, the Small Business Loan Fund. We thought we were making a smart move. After all, this program was designed to help banks lend more easily to local, small businesses trying to rebuild—exactly the lifeline our community needed. But the government turned us down, and, as I explained earlier, our new regulator was not in a position to vouch for us. It was a bit of a perfect storm, and the news hit us like a punch to the gut. We were left reeling, bewildered. We received whispers of the reason through back channels: *You have problems.* And the Treasury simply didn't want to invest in problem situations at that time.

Much of our frustration stemmed from our lack of access to information from the powers that be in DC. This was partly a function of our transition to the Office of the Comptroller of Currency (OCC). They proved to be an excellent regulator in the long run, and one that made us a better bank overall. However, like all new relationships, we didn't have the chance to establish mutual trust, so calls to their regional office, to get information about our situation and a path forward went unanswered. This was in stark contrast to our long, trusting relationship with our former regulator, the Office of Thrift Supervision (OTS). With the OTS, I could call their heads in DC and get a face-to-face meeting within days. A new relationship with a skeptical regulator at a troubling time was a major challenge for us, but one we methodically worked through. We slowly changed our attitudes and approach, and enlisted the help of a premier regulatory consulting firm Promontory Financial Group, acquired by IBM in 2016, to help us acclimate. The team at Promontory was terrific.

It's true, of course, that we had problems—everyone did, but we were climbing out of a shallower cellar, and better than most. The rejection from the US Treasury felt like a classic case of the bureaucratic machine applying a broad-brush approach. But we didn't let it get us down. Giants like JP Morgan Chase, PNC, and M&T loomed large, ready to seize on any misstep to attract our associates and customers. Instead, we embraced the challenge, recognizing that we had the organizational chutzpah to build our own program to make those small business loans. With the demise of Wilmington Trust, and our homegrown appeal, it was our responsibility to step and be Delaware's bank.

In the face of rejection, we were not going to wallow in self-pity, we were not going to gripe; we were going to move forward. It was then that I added an amplification to one of my favorite sayings, "Every cloud has a silver lining": *If you can't see it, find it; and if you can't find it, make it.* We were going to make a silver lining. Despite not having regulatory and government support, we rolled out our small business lending program with the vocal support of local politicians, and received great customer and market reaction. Our reputation, internal morale, and business prospects were all enhanced.

Lofty Goals

To lay out a clear road map for the next few years, my team and I had to zero-in on WSFS' most critical ambitions. What would the WSFS of the mid-2010s look like? Who did we aspire to become?

First on the list was the goal of routinely ranking among the top quintile of banks in the nation in financial performance—the top 20 percent. You might wonder why we didn't shoot for the top, say, 10 percent. It's because we understood the industry. Banks in that tier often tread dangerous waters, engaging in risky business that inevitably comes back to break them. Our experience taught us that a blend of aggressiveness and prudence was the key to sustained excellence.

We aimed for "sustainable high performance." This wasn't just a buzz term; it was about ensuring that our success wasn't a flash in the pan. In the banking world, sustainability means creating a virtuous cycle: We attract capital from investors; put that toward our people, products, and customers; and generate good profit. Then, we return some to the investors, and funnel the remainder into our company and community to grow—to generate greater returns and attract more investment. It's simple: *When we do well, our communities do well. When our communities do well, we do well.* We called that our "declaration of interdependence."

Finally, we needed a system of clarity and accountability. The best strategy to achieve that was to document our detailed plan and share it widely—to board members, investors, associates, customers, and community stakeholders who all needed to see our vision. Widespread transparency would keep us focused, honest, and on track as we pursued our ambitious goals.

The First "Good to Great" Years

When I think about this period in our journey, I like to invoke the book *Good to Great* by Jim Collins. True and lasting success, he writes, is rarely about one hit product, event, or year: it's the collective outcome of having the right people in the right roles, and putting in consistent effort and smart strategies over many years.

Over the pages of our 2013–2015 strategic plan booklet, we laid out our key goals for the next three years, and all the cascading division goals. We also posited four updated crucial pillars—mission, vision, strategy, and values—intended to carry WSFS into the post-crisis landscape. We'd spent months brainstorming as a leadership team; poring over the goals, their internal integrity, the words to use; trying to imbue each phrase with the right kind of meaning. We didn't want them to be typical, bland, incremental corporate platitudes that anybody could use. The document would, after all, be a playbook that would take the company through the next three years.

While other companies crafted their plans in the boardroom and kept them amongst their senior leadership team, our strategic plan was created in partnership with all associates, giving them a sense of ownership and responsibility over the bank's future. The mastermind behind that effort was Peggy, of course. Throughout the process of building and sharing the strategic plan, Peggy talked to all levels of associates and ran more than 40 workshops across the company, connecting with as many people as she could. *How do you see yourself and your work in the strategic plan?* she would ask associates. If they said they felt out of touch with the plan, Peggy would help them change their mindset, and come up with ways that they could make a difference. She's always had a particular genius for that kind of stuff.

We made a point of saying, "A strategic plan is only worthwhile if every associate can see themselves in it, and if it changes their behavior on a daily basis." That idea became so central to the bank's success that the new hire orientation for incoming associates was wrapped around the strategic plan, so everybody could be on the same page from day one. We made it very clear why we were doing what we were, and how each of our associates fit into our long-term strategy. After a while, almost every associate at WSFS knew the plan's key catchphrases by heart. We even tied their incentive compensation to their progress on the strategic plan—whatever their role. That really got everyone moving in the same direction, working towards the same goals.

Every quarter, our leadership team measured the company's progress toward the strategic objectives that had been outlined in the plan, and then communicated their findings to the associates, the board, and investors. While that sounds like a simple, straightforward approach, it's not something many companies do. We got a lot of praise from associates who liked knowing what the goals were, how the progress was going, and what they could do in their day-to-day roles that had a direct impact.

Company outsiders also applauded our efforts. We had investors come up to us effectively saying, *We love you guys. You're the only company that says, "Here's what we plan to do, in detail; here's how we did it; here's what's working, what's not, and how we're going to adjust."* While the financial crisis was in the rearview mirror, the distrust it had sowed in financial institutions continued to reverberate throughout the market. By being focused, detailed, and transparent on plans and goals, we hoped to reestablish trust, and help WSFS stand out from the crowd.

There would be no big talk about our potential future results without credible plans, actions, accountability, and transparency behind it. We'd learned this practice years earlier, when it felt like we were surrounded by banks engaging in big-and-splashy but vague marketing efforts—but we waited to roll out the "We Stand for Service" brand campaign to the wider market until we had enough traction for insiders and outsiders to say, "Yes, that's true, and they do it better than others." We fundamentally believed in the sequential integrity of thoughts, words, actions, habits, and destiny.

"Talentship" and "Winnovation"

During these years, we again turned our focus to the essential items for realizing the ambitious goals outlined in our 2013–2015 strategic plan. At WSFS, we firmly believe that a company's strength lies in its people, making talent development a cornerstone of our discussions. During every quarterly meeting and strategic offsite, we grappled with fundamental questions: Who are our next leaders, our top performers? Who are the irreplaceable contributors driving our success? How can we ensure their ongoing engagement and growth?

Advancing our talented individuals was not just important; it was imperative. We recognized the necessity of proper succession planning to guarantee that there would always be capable leaders ready to step into key roles in a growing, changing organization. Additionally, we embarked on a rigorous overhaul of our recruiting processes, an initiative championed by Peggy.

Our partnership with Gallup played a crucial role in tracking our progress in people engagement, utilizing the Human Sigma model to understand the vital intersection and combined power of associate engagement and customer advocacy. We encapsulated these efforts under the banner of "Talentship."

Simultaneously, we embraced a concept we termed "Winnovation," a proactive strategy designed to keep us at the forefront of industry advancements. With the rapid rise of smartphones in the early 2010s, it became imperative for financial institutions to enhance customer engagement through mobile platforms. To facilitate this, we established a dedicated "Winnovation" office, led by Jen Jurden and her agile team. Their mission was clear: What should WSFS be doing more of, better? What should our next steps be? We wanted to make sure that as we were growing, we were growing with quality and efficiency. We didn't want to just throw spaghetti at the wall; we wanted to be tracking who—in our industry and others—were doing things better, and how we could learn from them.

Jen and her team affirmed that WSFS would have to move towards a more fee-based business model—customers paying us fees for value-added services was much better than the shrinking-margin, commodity business of making loans or taking deposits. Next, the team identified WSFS' investments in Cash Connect for ATMs, and wealth management services, as other key drivers of growth, encouraging the bank to keep pursuing ways to get involved in those sectors. Third, the team acknowledged that

WSFS had to improve the quality of the assets on its books, and improve efficiency throughout the organization. There would be no sloppy investing and spending; no balance-sheet time bombs or every-few-years disruptive restructurings.

We kept busy with a crop of home-grown ideas. WSFS started Mobile Cash—which allowed customers to get cash fast by flashing their phones at an ATM. We were one of the first banks in the country to do something like that. WSFS Everyday Pay allowed customers to easily transfer money on their mobile apps from one person to another, like Venmo and Zelle, which popped up around the same time. And within Cash Connect, an initiative called SmartSafe allowed retailers who put a lot of cash in their store safes to keep it more secure, and get instant bank credit for it. This innovative effort was led by Tom Stevenson and his team, who constantly worked to make our Cash Connect business more relevant and profitable.

Then, in 2014, an unexpected call from Delaware Governor Jack Markell and Senator Tom Carper presented us with a unique opportunity. The call centered on Arkadi Kuhlmann, founder of ING Direct, which had been the leading internet-only bank in the US. Once headquartered in Wilmington, it had to be sold by their Dutch holding company due to the parent company's government bailout.

Through his start-up Zenbanx, Arkadi had a vision in US mobile banking: he raised $50 million to develop a platform where people could do their banking and engage with social media in the same place. In an innovative twist, users could deposit money in one currency, and have it translated to other currencies—a real convenience for people who did a lot of foreign travel and transactions. What Arkadi still needed, however, was a banking partner and a charter to get to market. Recognizing our historical ties to Delaware, and reputation for partnering with outside management teams, Markell and Carper saw WSFS as an ideal collaborator.

Through strategic teamwork, and the lessons learned from our past joint ventures, we helped Arkadi establish Zenbanx in Delaware, resulting in hundreds of new jobs—a true win-win-win scenario. Our investment in Zenbanx ultimately yielded around $10 million dollars in gain, as it was sold to SoFi in 2016, and it provided us invaluable insights into the fast-evolving frontier of mobile banking.

We were committed to staying within our strategy *and* keeping up with the rapidly changing landscape.

Measuring and Managing

As our WSFS team pursued our goals, tracking and recording our progress became a science. Quarterly reports demonstrated clearly what we were doing right, and where we could improve. Yearly analyses helped refine our aims. We became obsessed with measuring and managing our goals and outcomes.

The 2014 annual report was the first fully fledged example of the kind of information WSFS associates, customers, investors, and other constituents could glean from the bank's internal studies. It was packed with financial statistics—black and white proof that our strategies were working.

One of the numbers I was most proud of within the report

was the bank's Core Return on Average Assets—ROA. In 2009, our ROA was essentially 0; by 2012, it had slogged back to .73 percent. In 2013, it was 1.07 percent; and in 2014, it had climbed to 1.17 percent. This was a massive move forward in just a few years, and it put WSFS squarely on the path towards that coveted top 20 percent of our peers' performance. By 2014, we were outperforming the broader economy; we were out-performing our peers; we were taking market share organically and through acquisitions.

A Top-Quintile Bank

I've found that it takes an organization a generation to create and execute a good business model. By 2015, WSFS' strategic plan, started in the early 2000s and severely interrupted by the financial crisis and Great Recession, was in full swing and yield-ing results: The bank was indisputably on the road to sustainable high performance. We were also officially a top-quintile bank.

Our success didn't feel like a fluke. Every facet of our busi-ness was healthy and performing. We weren't relying on a sin-gle division's success while others lagged behind, nor were we buoyed by risky products or ventures, or external factors like a bubble economy or tax cuts. Instead, we achieved this enviable position through solid balance sheet and expense management; diversified revenue sources; customers that paid us a premium for our service; organic growth; internal innovations; and small, synergistic partnerships and acquisitions—together, a strong foundation for future success.

This was the moment when our engine truly began to hum, propelling us forward in a robust and healthy manner. We remained steadfast in strengthening the culture that underpinned our strength. Leaders like Peggy and Sheila, along with their dedicated teams, were consistently raising the bar, pushing us to explore new heights of excellence.

As we tracked our progress on Total Shareholder Return, the WSFS edge was unmistakable. Anyone who'd bought stock in the few years after the financial crisis had more than doubled, tripled, and in some cases, even quadrupled their investment by the end of 2015.

Yet, there was still much more to do, and much more to come.

SIXTEEN | IF I'M NOT LEARNING, I'M DYING

By Mark Turner

WSFS' significant advances in the mid-2010s sprang from an intense period of exploration, creativity, growth, and success at the company. Things felt solid. But outside the bank's halls, we could see the world changing once again.

I knew the currents were shifting when I attended Money20/20: the next generation's answer to financial conferences of years past. Unlike traditional industry get-togethers like Acquire or Be Acquired, which tended to draw about 2,000 seasoned US bankers and professionals to Arizona each year, Money20/20 pulled a crowd of more than 10,000, mostly younger creators from over 75 countries. They all descended on Las Vegas for a days-long extravaganza that revolved around the future of, well, money—mostly in terms of digitization and the smartphone.

With the city's glitz as a backdrop, people of all stripes mixed and mingled, discussing the biggest up-and-coming forces in the industry, like the growing opportunities in fintech—"financial technology" companies—and neobanks, which operated exclusively online without traditional branch networks. Both could disrupt banking as we knew it. In order to keep our nearly

200-year legacy going, WSFS would have to change too. We knew we'd have to embrace the social media age, and find ways to better serve customers anywhere, anytime, online. We hoped doing this would help us grow as a full-service organization with robust retail banking, commercial banking, wealth management, and ancillary businesses.

With all this transition afoot, I also knew that one last, big thing would eventually have to change at the bank: its leader.

The Next Blueprint

I was never going to be CEO at WSFS forever. Back in 2013, I'd surprised quite a few board members with the news that I was putting an end date on my time at WSFS: six more years, two more turns of the strategic plan. I felt like that would give me a concrete goal, and enough time to truly help the bank reach best-in-class, and sustainable high-performance, before passing the torch on to the company's next leader—who I already believed was likely to be Rodger Levenson.

In the years that followed, the board and I worked subtly towards that date: giving Rodger increasing responsibilities, transitioning some of his roles, and thinking about what we wanted WSFS to look like when it was finally time for me to hand it off. While I hadn't officially announced my plans to associates or other key WSFS team members, I wanted to get the wheels turning early.

In a letter that accompanied the 2016–2018 strategic plan, I spelled out three core areas where the bank would continue to focus its energy: acquisitions/partnerships, innovation, and talent. I asked Rodger to lead the Corporate Development department—another umbrella term for mergers, acquisitions, and partnerships—where his task would be identifying new opportunities and executing on them; growing the bank while further broadening his network, experiences, and skills. WSFS was still looking to expand further into southeastern Pennsylvania, and we also wanted to grow laterally in sectors that would be complementary to banking, like wealth advisory firms and family offices.

While he was busy charting a course for that, I took stock. Some executives would have been satisfied with coming in to work each day with a mission to keep things humming along. But I'm not wired that way. If I'm not learning and growing, I'm dying.

Every year since 1999, I had done a pretty extensive executive education program—whether an MBA; going away for a week to the Aspen Institute or the Center for Creative Leadership; or Harvard, or Penn, or Berkeley; or CEO roundtables like Anat Bird's SuperCommunity Bank Forums—I made it a routine part of my ongoing development. But by 2016, I was running out of fresh educational endeavors, and I started to wonder: Could I come up with a learning experience of my own?

I considered my wife Regina's career as a professor at the University of Pennsylvania. The idea of taking a sabbatical was a well-entrenched part of academic life, allowing educators to take time off from their regular jobs to learn from experts elsewhere. Could I do something similar? The concept was nearly unheard of in the business sector, but I couldn't shake the feeling that I had to look outside our walls to learn how to meet the particular challenges of the next generation. Millennials were overtaking boomers; the smartphone was becoming the new bank branch; and about 2,500 platforms had sprung up in fintech and neo-banks, helping customers pay bills, deposit funds, take out loans, and manage their wealth. Were they going to overtake banking? Become a passing fad? Or just meld into the banking environment? I needed to talk to other business leaders about how they were tackling this list of consequential questions.

Charting an Unconventional Course

As I began sketching out my plan for a "sabbatical," I quickly hit a wall: there were no role models, no blueprints. I'd have to make my own way.

When I met with the board to explain what I wanted to do, the members fell into three camps. A few leaned in—notably the progressive ones like Skip, CG, Anat, and J.J.—saying, "Go for it!" Others hovered in neutral territory, offering the reassuring, "We trust you, Mark." And then there were the skeptics, who were not opposed but were certainly uneasy.

I couldn't blame them. My proposal was an anomaly in the conservative world of banking, and their traditional instincts kicked in. Questions flew: "What's the return on this investment?" "A CEO taking three months away, what will the investors think?" "What about the associates? Who will run the bank? How do we even begin to manage that?"

The three months I was proposing seemed to them like a lifetime, especially when I planned to sever all ties with WSFS during my absence. I wanted to be completely unplugged—out of sight, out of mind. It was a radical leap, and I was asking them to trust me and my team.

Luckily, there was a capable and willing leader ready to step up to the plate. I asked the board to let Rodger take over while I was away. "This is a test of the organization after me: a test of Rodger, of your belief in Rodger, and a test of the team's ability to step up," I said. By this point, I'd already told many key people that I'd be leaving the executive ranks by 2020. This was the bank's unique chance to really test its succession plan—and while I was still around, just in case.

When I put it in those terms, all board members were eventually convinced. They'd get to really experience Rodger's leadership abilities and potential, and I assured them I'd bring a lot of valuable information back about the sea changes going on in the industry. I think they felt further confidence when they saw that associates and analysts weren't rattled as we broached the idea with them. And so a blueprint took shape for my "Leading Practices Tour," a months-long cross-country journey during which I'd visit a variety of business trailblazers, gleaning kernels of wisdom that I could take back to strengthen and even fundamentally change WSFS.

Who would I visit? I used my own network, our partners' networks, and the board's connections. Ben Brake, David Turner, Thère du Pont, and Chris Gheysens—newer, younger, more digitally savvy members who had joined the board in our recent reformation—were especially helpful. We ultimately identified about 110 companies that were doing inspiring things, and I drafted a letter to each of their leaders. I shared who I was, what challenges WSFS faced, and said *I want to come and learn from you.*

I thought maybe I'd get back a handful of affirmative responses, but I ultimately wound up scheduling a remarkable 49 visits—some lasting a few hours, others lasting a few days. While many companies agreed to host me, others took it a step further, recommending additional companies and executives for me to visit. And then there were a number of companies that said, "We'd like to visit you, too."

The Leading Practices Tour officially began in August 2016, when I literally unplugged from my C-suite office and headed to my first stop, meeting CEOs of prominent start-ups in the digital platform lending space. WSFS and I would never be the same.

On the Road

Though I technically planned to be unreachable during my travels, I promised everyone at WSFS that I'd update them weekly in the form of a blog—where I'd detail my visits and outline some of my biggest takeaways, triumphs, and tribulations. In my very first post on July 27th, 2016, I included a picture of our family cat, sitting on top of our home AV stack.

The accompanying picture captures a little bit of how I feel, I wrote. *Weenie has wandered into an area he doesn't quite belong, out of curiosity and naiveté. He's out of place in the tech world...yet wide-eyed, and determined, and ready to spring into action.*

Anxious, excited, ready for adventure and outside my comfort zone, my first destination was New York City, where I'd be attending panel discussions with the founders of several digital lender start-ups: including Aaron Vermut, the CEO of Prosper;

and Sam Graziano, the CEO of Fundation. After that, my tour would take me to North Jersey; Texas; Colorado; Washington, DC; the Midwest; Boston; New York (again); San Francisco; Silicon Valley; Las Vegas; and Aspen.

As energizing, fascinating, and inspiring as it all was, I quickly learned that life as a traveling CEO on a long mission was not a walk in the park. Lonely hotel rooms blurred into one another; punctuated by fast, unhealthy meals; and quick stops along long stretches of road, leaving little time for exercise. Mental fatigue set in as I prepared extensively for each meeting, striving to sound somewhat informed in what often felt like a series of blind sales calls. It became an exhausting endeavor for a natural introvert like me. But instead of retreating into my shell, I had to be an energetic, enthusiastic, and outgoing sponge—asking all the big questions and soaking up key takeaways.

For the last many years of my career, I was accustomed to having things come to me, to being in control and well-informed. This experience flipped that dynamic completely; I found myself unfamiliar with the people and companies around me, their work, and how they operated. Suddenly, I was the one asking questions, required to embody curiosity and knee-bending humility.

The discussions were made a bit easier by the fact that both parties had chosen to participate. Every visit was the result of a collaborative effort with the company I was visiting—a win-win where we could both learn more about each other. I found out that people on the leading edge of things *like* talking about what they do and their successes. They enjoy sharing, passing on wisdom and knowledge, and engaging in a back-and-forth about the future.

As I logged miles, one woman was working behind the scenes to make sure it all went as smoothly as possible: Kathy Quinn, my executive assistant, whose effort was invaluable in making my tour a success. She helped the tour flow geographically—structuring visits according to states and coasts, and also building in weekends for me to go home to spend time with Regina, and my daughters, Becky and Katie. This was key time that I needed to recenter, reconnect, and recharge. "He always looked like he was so darn tired through the whole thing," Kathy recalls about me with a laugh. "It was a lot of work, but it was fun, too, because I did all the nitty gritty—the airlines, contacting people."

The executive team at WSFS mostly heeded my instructions to refrain from contact unless there was a problem that only I could solve. They reached out substantively only once, and that was in the wake of a major scandal involving another bank, Wells Fargo. The San Francisco–based institution was found to have opened fake, unauthorized accounts for millions of customers, driven by extreme pressure on employees to meet unrealistic sales targets. As a result, many of their employees created false records and enrolled customers in products they never wanted.

It was a tremendous breach of trust, and the fallout was dramatic. Wells Fargo had to publicly apologize, and fork over multiple massive settlements in the years that followed. Regulators capped their growth, and two senior executives—former CEO John Stumpf, and ex-Head of Community Bank Carrie Tolstedt—were banned from the banking industry and made to pay millions in penalties. As the ripple effects reverberated throughout the industry, banks all over the country were placed under a magnifying glass once again.

So, during the tour, I had to attend a board meeting by phone, to reassure board members that there were no signs of this practice at WSFS. We would still conduct our own investigations to examine our practices, but I confidently said I believed that we never product-pushed or opened fake accounts. (Our subsequent investigations revealed that we had not).

Beyond that one interaction, everyone at WSFS "connected" with me through my blog. I found it to be a very helpful way for me to reflect each week, making it easier to identify key lessons and revelations amid the nonstop traveling. But it also had the unintended consequence of bringing me closer than ever to my associates—many of whom later told me that they felt they truly got to know me through my weekly updates.

As great an experience as it has been, I am also really looking forward to getting back and working with all of you, I wrote in the blog's November 1st update. *I have missed my family at home, and my family at the bank.*

After 49 visits, more than three months, and 44,000 miles, it was finally time for me to come home to WSFS and start synthesizing and implementing what I'd learned.

I'd visited massive technology companies like Apple, Google, and Twilio; innovative banks like Northern Trust and Eastern Bank; start-ups like Lending Club, Plaid, Digital Asset Holdings; and more traditional businesses like Wawa, Becton Dickinson, DaVita, and Walmart. While most were vastly different from each other, their respective successes were largely rooted in the following: strong cultures; visible, visionary, and constructive leaders; a deep understanding of their customers' desires; continual innovation; and programs for employee growth and organizational learning.

Being away for so long made me realize more than ever just how capable the other members on my executive team were. I was hoping that this would be the case, but they really blew me away—in my absence, they'd more than stepped up to the plate, taking on extra responsibility, and making key decisions to ensure that WSFS didn't skip a beat. In fact, while I was away, the team closed one critical acquisition, and signed the papers for two more.

I left for the tour as a leader of people, and I came back as a leader of leaders. Now, it would be easier for me to empower my team for even greater company success.

Lasting Impacts

It's hard to fully express just how important and influential my Leading Practices Tour was—both for the bank, and for my own life. The lessons I learned on my unconventional "sabbatical" of sorts went on to shape the bank's internal workings and culture, propelling new initiatives and strategies; while also emphasizing to associates that out-of-the-box thinking, entrepreneurship, and curiosity were encouraged and celebrated at our company.

As a direct result of the tour, we created, among other things, a customer experience department; implemented a new leadership development program; added a new life-balancing benefit for associates; appreciated fully the need to partner with fintechs for our R&D and growth in exploratory areas; and committed, in the right way at the right time, to dramatically rebalance our banking delivery—reducing our physical infrastructure, and investing heavily in digital delivery for the future of WSFS.

The tour also had an outsize external impact, reaching farther than I believed it could. Once people outside the organization found out about my tour, I wound up getting lots of calls, saying things like, *Wow, can you come tell us about this?* I've been asked to speak at dozens of executive forums and banking conferences about what I did, why I did it, how I did it, the lessons learned, and strategies employed.

The following points are routinely a part of those discussions: "How does an old organization learn new things?" "How can a CEO unplug and leave his desk for months to travel across the country?" "How did a 'leadership sabbatical' become the perfect succession test?"

The tour was a unique and powerful initiative for what we learned, and how it changed the bank. Furthermore, the board and I were even more confident in Rodger's potential. Still, I had a few years left in my leadership at WSFS, and I was even more determined to make the most of them.

SEVENTEEN | BECOMING PART OF WSFS

By Pat Ward, as told to Brittany Kriegstein. Pat was CEO of Penn Liberty Bank from 2004–2016, and joined WSFS in 2016, after the merger.

While Mark was embarking on his cross-country travels, a crucial event was unfolding back at WSFS that would shape the bank's strategy for years to come—and I was at the center of it.

Penn Liberty was a community bank headquartered in Wayne, Pennsylvania, and I'd been the leader there since 2004. By June of 2016, we had grown to over $700 million in assets. The place was really like a family, and we initially weren't looking to sell it, but we came around because we knew it was the best possible decision for our partners. The only problem: I knew it would be hard to find an acquiring organization that I'd feel I could trust. As I said, Penn Liberty was like a family—I absolutely *had* to make sure everybody landed on their feet.

As whispers of that upcoming decision made their way around the banking market, a number of bank CEOs started calling me. One of the few that gave me a good feeling was Mark Turner. We'd actually met back when he was on the mergers and acquisitions team at Meridian Bank, so I'd known him for a long time. WSFS and Penn Liberty had similar cultures: Both were intent on being helpful to community organizations, and both were very generous in supporting nonprofits and community volunteering. The biggest difference, really, was that WSFS had an extra zero on its balance sheet. I knew Mark would do everything in his power not to break up my family.

From the start of our conversations, Mark was transparent and open with me. WSFS had successfully completed six acquisitions since 2008, and it didn't take me long to understand why they were good at it. First, they had a relationship between their strategy and culture that was uniquely solid: They pursued acquisitions for the future good of the company, and used their strong culture to bring new employees into the fold. Second, working with Mark meant I knew what to expect. He was genuine when he said he couldn't make any specific promises but would do what he could to keep as many of my employees as possible.

Luckily, Penn Liberty was mostly outside of WSFS' footprint, so the bank needed many of my employees to stay on to continue running those branches and offices. It was an exciting time, and a major relief for me. Honesty and integrity are hard to come by in these kinds of transactions, but Mark delivered on everything he promised. That's hard to do. I'd had some really negative experiences with acquisitions in the past, but WSFS was just so different. Almost all our staff members who weren't ready for retirement found continued employment.

Why was it important for WSFS to be a good acquirer? Because acquisitions would ultimately help the company grow toward sustainable high performance. But it was equally important to acquire the *right* companies—places that would align with WSFS' core cultural values, and further help its customer base while bringing some great new associates into the ranks. WSFS used its strategy and culture as a two-pronged approach, tackling acquisitions from both sides to ensure a smooth and dignified transition for all.

On August 17, 2016, a story in the *Delaware Business Times* shared the breaking news: The acquisition was complete. Penn Liberty bank accounts had been successfully converted to WSFS bank accounts, and all former Penn Liberty customers would have full access to WSFS banking services moving forward. All Penn Liberty branches would reopen under WSFS branding. And the former CEO of Penn Liberty—me, Patrick J. Ward—would be joining the WSFS board of directors, and assuming the roles of executive vice president and Pennsylvania market president.

As of this writing, I'm still at WSFS, because Penn Liberty was such a similar place that it made sense to stay. I've served as executive vice president of our Pennsylvania market, and spent a few years on the board, so I can say that the bank's commitment to customer service is sincere. It's not an advertising ploy. We continue to be really focused on the local market, and we're very invested in this region—not spread all over the country. We're also still incredibly dedicated to volunteering and giving: With WSFS charitable foundations that directly support our customers, millions of dollars that could have paid dividends or lined our own pockets go back into the community. It's just the right thing to do, plain and simple.

During Skip's tenure, he was really fighting for the bank to survive. But the broader community stretch was Mark's work. Coming from North Philly, he's a local guy, and local people could see how committed he was to them. I think that's one reason we've done so well in the Pennsylvania and Philadelphia markets.

The next few years would see WSFS really come into its own as a place that other banking and wealth companies felt comfortable merging with. Of course, there were ups and downs. However, through it all, the bank leaned hard on its values: service, integrity, honesty, and respect. If those sound like easy virtues to maintain in a fast-growing company, think again.

EIGHTEEN | MERGERS AND ACQUISITIONS

By Mark Turner

Acquisitions are not for the faint-hearted; they involve complex dynamics where one company absorbs another, reshaping the combined organization's structure and future. As the entity expands, some employees rise through the ranks while others face the harsh reality of being let go. Common wisdom says that more than half of business combinations destroy value. When we embarked on crafting our acquisition strategy, we were driven by a singular objective: to outperform every other player.

Why chase this elusive goal? The answer was simple: it would unlock crucial opportunities and add key talent, like Pat Ward, firmly within our fold. We envisioned a reputation so robust that when other companies considered selling, they'd think, "Let's talk to WSFS." Our strategy involved not just adding assets, but impressing other banks—turning them into part of our potential client base—which required a deft touch. Success depended on an excellent strategy, but also on an infrastructure and culture that could support it—a combination demanding constant vigilance and effort.

Our significant push into acquisitions really started in 2010, during the pang of the Great Recession, with the purchase of Christiana Bank & Trust: a strategic move that bolstered our wealth management capabilities by adding vital brand, talent, and operational systems.

Convincing people to trust a new entity with their financial assets, especially when dealing with generational family wealth, is no small feat. Christiana had a long-standing, local reputation as an excellent name in wealth management that catapulted our own languishing internal efforts.

A flurry of acquisitions ensued, with WSFS completing 10 between 2008 and 2022. Each successive acquisition was a building block, allowing us to tackle larger, more complex deals. On several occasions, companies called us outright to privately negotiate a deal instead of going through an acquisition auction. In other cases, WSFS was on a very short list of institutions contacted for a limited auction process. The momentum was undeniable, but the questions loomed large: Did we possess the horsepower to sustain this pace? And, were these efforts translating into real gains in our franchise value? We wanted to continue to grow, and add capabilities, improve our profitability, and diversify our revenue. Our strategy hinged on identifying and skillfully integrating excellent opportunities.

The Value of Pricing Discipline, Due Diligence, Good Relationships, and Good Contracts

Our acquisition of Christiana Bank & Trust had many quirks, twists, and turns. We tried to acquire it in 2007, for $65 million, but lost in a bidding war to National Penn Bank. However, National Penn's fortunes and management changed in 2010—as did many banks'—during the Great Recession. At that time, they looked to streamline their operations, and they put Christiana back on the blocks. We bid once more at a price that made sense at that time, and were again outbid. But the deal ultimately came back to us because National Penn's CFO, who I had worked with earlier at Meridian Bank, did not trust the winning bidder; and we, on the other hand, had a good, trusting relationship. The net price this time was about $30 million, less than half of what the company sold for three years earlier. Discipline, patience, good relationships—and the courage to do a deal during an uncertain time—paid off for us in many ways.

But the process still wasn't over. We ran into a last-minute misunderstanding among investment bankers on how the net asset sale price would be calculated when we excluded certain loans that National Penn wanted to hold onto. Both sides dug in on their position, imperiling a deal that was good for both companies. On the last weekend possible, their CFO and I negotiated a fair settlement, on a Saturday morning over coffee at a McDonald's between our homes. I cannot stress enough the paramount importance of cultivating trusting relationships—in business and in life.

On top of that, during due diligence, we uncovered some risky business that Christiana had administered with Stranger-Owned Life Insurance trusts—arrangements wherein a group of investors could purchase life insurance policies for people with whom they had no prior relationship. As we dug into it, we concluded we had no way of evaluating its risks and ultimate liability. As a result, we negotiated a full indemnification for Christiana's businesses prior to our ownership. This proved prescient and valuable, as we were able to put a few pieces of business, and their losses, back to the seller; it saved us over $20 million (on a $30 million deal), and again, protected our good reputation in the marketplace.

Small Victories

As 2010 came to a close, and the ink dried on our deal with Christiana Bank & Trust, we decided we should raise still more capital—in part to help pay for the acquisition, and in part to gird ourselves for what may come in a still tenuous economy. We turned to our good investment banking partners, Sandler O'Neill, CEO Jimmy Dunne; and Head of Investment Banking, Brian Sterling to help get it done.

After the initial required filings and building interest, Rodger, Steve Fowle, and I headed to NYC, hoping to get a good price and close the deal on a capital raise. The day and night were spent talking with potential investors on conference calls and in group meetings, answering questions, building the final book, and negotiating pricing—an iterative process that depends on many interested parties coming to agreement. We had drafted a board resolution that said management couldn't close the deal until a subcommittee of the board approved its final price—a disciplined backstop that would allow us to hold firm against the pressures of the moment and the market. Skip, CG, Cal Morgan, and Ted were on this committee.

During uncertain times like these, it's typical for a secondary stock offering to be priced below the previous closing share price. This makes sense, as new shares can dilute the value for existing shareholders, especially when we're seeking additional capital to support higher-risk initiatives. We anticipated this discount, and everything seemed to be going according to plan until something unexpected occurred. Nick Adams, a successful, reputable bank investor who knew us very well, called into the room and asked to speak with me alone. That itself was unusual. He said he wanted the whole deal and was willing to pay a premium.

This was a bit of a shock to everyone. For a variety of reasons, we couldn't accept his proposal, but we realized that we could give him a big piece of the deal, and use his offer to pull all the pricing up. Ted especially pushed us to hold firm at the best pricing. When word spread that Nick was in the deal in a big way, and at a premium, other potential investors gained more confidence and had to raise their bids to stay in the process.

In 1998, as one of my first acts as WSFS CFO, again with Jimmy Dunne and Sandler O'Neill's expert help, we raised capital in the first-ever variable-rate, trust-preferred share offering by a single issuer. This time, Sandler stayed with us until well past midnight, and helped close the $50 million common stock deal at a premium to the prior day's closing price. This was the only bank capital raise in 2010 that had achieved that milestone. It was another first for WSFS with Sandler's help. During a challenging time, we welcomed those small wins.

On the Map

By the mid-2010s, our acquisitions gained significant market attention. In 2013, we took in Array Financial Group, Inc. (and the related Arrow Land Transfer Company). They were a high-end, boutique mortgage business in nearby Haverford, Pennsylvania, with an excellent reputation for service, especially in unusual situations. With them, we picked up a bevy of top talent, including Jeff Ruben, the company's president, who would soon transform our entire mortgage operations to best-in-class. In 2014, we merged with a small community bank near Dover, Delaware: First National Bank of Wyoming. And in 2015, we acquired Alliance Bank in southeastern PA, and then signed our contract with Penn Liberty Bank—making it a breakout period for WSFS' progress in the highly desirable Philly suburbs of Montgomery, Chester, and Delaware counties.

Executing one acquisition is tough; pulling off three or four in a short period is even harder. But the organization was in high gear. With a wealth of talent, sustained success, and a harmonious culture and strategy, we felt we could maintain momentum. I'm glad we had that can-do attitude, because our winning streak solidified our reputation as a leading growth company and an "acquirer of choice." Most crucially, it positioned us on the threshold of Philadelphia proper, a coveted market—though we still had to build further trust.

In 2016, the pace accelerated. While I was away on the Leading Practices Tour, the news broke that WSFS had acquired Powdermill Financial Solutions, based in Greenville, Delaware. Founded in 2003 by members of the well-known du Pont family, Powdermill was a trusted multi-family office known for managing substantial wealth—a place where such households could go to help take care of investments, insurance, trusts, taxes, bills, and more.

A few weeks later, our acquisition of Penn Liberty went into effect, with Pat Ward's family of associates joining the WSFS clan. And two months after that, we went public with news that we'd acquired West Capital Management—a Philly-based registered investment advisory (RIA) that also offered wealth management services to burgeoning high-net worth individuals. I would say that all the companies perceived these acquisitions as mutually advantageous. Each organization gained access to our client base, while we were positioned to offer banking services to their high-caliber customers.

By now, WSFS was operating at near-peak effectiveness. The pieces were aligning, and we could feel ourselves evolving into the regional, full-service, high-touch player we aspired to be. Other important highlights from 2016 included the bank's venture with Jerry Schiano to invest in home equity lender Spring EQ, which promised to modernize the antiquated, paper-heavy, face-to-face process of home lending.

Yet, Philadelphia proper—my hometown, and the largest and most competitive nearby market—remained elusive. Did we have what it would take to break into this critical city?

Beneficial Indeed: The WSFS of Philly

Expanding into Philadelphia itself was a logical next step, as we'd maximized our potential around Delaware by this point. But our capital base limited our lending capacity in Philly. Further, as I wrapped up the Leading Practices Tour, we concluded we needed more capital, cost savings, and organizational drive to support our robust digital investment plans. Fortunately, our stellar performance over previous years had attracted numerous companies interested in aligning with us. The challenge now was to find the perfect partner in Philly to help us stake our claim as a major player in this market filled with opportunity.

It didn't take long for us to find a potential fit in 159-year-old Beneficial Bank, a venerable institution headquartered in the heart of the city. With a rich history and similar values, they were us, in Philly. Yet, despite the shared culture, Beneficial struggled to meet expectations for growth and profitability; not unusual for a newly public company facing intense pressure to deliver returns. They had quietly explored their alternatives and, as fate would have it, knew our management team. They felt WSFS might be just the right partner.

The call came in early 2018: Gerry Cuddy, Beneficial's CEO, wanted to talk. We met at the Union League in Philadelphia, and started to have some serious discussions. Even though the surface gleamed with potential, the underlying complexities were daunting. Since we were of similar asset size, I was worried about the prospect of doing a "merger of equals"—where both companies share leadership and board responsibilities, half from one, half from the other. Such mergers sound like corporate heaven.

But in practice, they're usually messy, and often fraught with strife as companies grapple for clarity and dominance. You futz around for two or three years, trying to figure things out, until you realize the inevitable—which is that the organization, to be successful, needs one dominant leadership team; one dominant board; and one dominant strategy and culture. As good a plan as it might seem when both CEOs sit down and talk about splitting the most critical functions of an organization, I've never seen it play out well.

Gerry understood my reservations and was refreshingly honest about Beneficial's situation. He effectively said, *You guys have the better leadership team, board, business model, and strategy.* He had some demands of his own: He asked if his management team could stay on through the transition, and he wanted to keep a few board seats. Those were reasonable asks, allowing us to consider the acquisition seriously.

But the numbers told a story of their own. When my team analyzed the situation through a traditional M&A model perspective, they found a big obstacle. The cost savings from eliminating redundant locations and positions were insufficient to meet Beneficial's price expectations. Still, I saw a slew of net positives that the acquisition could bring to the new WSFS. I considered how to get around the cons, and asked the team not to look at it like a traditional acquisition. I asked instead, *What would we do if we were building the combined company from scratch, for the future of banking?* This shift in perspective was crucial. We needed to see things differently and go deeper, be more transformative.

With offices and people throughout Philadelphia and South Jersey, Beneficial would give WSFS the geographical breadth we wanted. As the industry was moving away from brick-and-mortar bank branches, I saw a crucial window of opportunity: If we closed about one-third of our combined physical outposts, we could retain our shared client base and WSFS could instead invest much of that cost savings in a new infrastructure for digital delivery. This new technology was much needed for internal efficiency, and much desired by customers for running their financial lives; and doing the deal this way could still make it work financially for both buyer and seller.

When we went public with that plan, we got a lot of push-back from analysts and investors who thought it was too risky for a bank our size to invest so boldly in big location cuts and new digital delivery. But we forged ahead with confidence. On August 8, 2018, we officially announced the groundbreaking news: WSFS would be combining with Beneficial Bancorp, Inc. in a transaction valued around $1.5 billion. With about $14 billion in assets and growing, we'd become the largest locally headquartered bank for the Greater Delaware Valley, the market with the sixth-largest deposit concentration in the country. It would get us into the heart of Philly, and double our asset size.

While I was the architect behind the plan, I knew I wouldn't be the one ultimately implementing the important changes on the ground to make everything run smoothly. That person, of course, was Rodger, still learning the leadership ropes as my days as WSFS CEO wound down.

He was understandably nervous. Working out the internal marching orders for such a large acquisition would have been challenging for any leader, let alone one who had just started the job. Rodger was quick to approach me, saying that if I wanted to delay the process of our leadership transition so I could finish up with Beneficial, he would understand.

But I was resolute. He was ready. Based on my experience guiding the company through the financial crisis, it actually helps for the new CEO to sink their teeth into something big to build their own leadership chops and style. And besides, I'd still be around as executive chair to help him navigate if the waters got rough. He knew I was there for WSFS and for him.

On March 1, 2019, the deal was official, and the marketplace took note. Many much bigger banks would eventually copy our intrepid plans to close physical locations and use that money to fund digital delivery. This strategy, of using a big acquisition to remake the company for the future—taking a whiteboard approach and disinvesting in physical delivery while reinvesting in digital delivery—was born out of the lessons I learned from my Leading Practices Tour just two years earlier. Along with our forays into business banking and wealth management, this was the biggest strategic move we made in the prior 20 years.

After the dust settled, WSFS essentially became a dual-head-quartered institution: with one at 500 Delaware Avenue in Wilmington, and the other at 1818 Market Street in Philadelphia. At $1.5 billion, it was by far our largest merger to date, and the sight of our bright green WSFS sign, radiant from the top of the new building in Center City Philadelphia, was a striking symbol of our growth and prominence.

Still, there was more in store.

Bryn Mawr Trust—
A Wealth Management Powerhouse

The foundation for a merger with Bryn Mawr Trust was being carefully constructed as early as 2015. This groundwork was not laid in boardrooms or high-rise offices, but over dinners I shared with their CEO, Frank Leto, in a Japanese restaurant on West Chester Pike: a midpoint between our homes. While I often made time to talk to other leaders in the banking industry—mostly to talk about potential business opportunities and occasionally to commiserate—my meetings with Frank, held a couple times each year, were more a strategic dialogue between two men at the helm of similar enterprises, driven by common values and goals.

We had a growing, mutual understanding of the pressures and possibilities inherent in our respective operations. We broached the subject of merging our organizations multiple times, though the merger never materialized during my tenure as CEO. It was clear, however, that in the wake of our acquisition of Beneficial, Bryn Mawr Trust saw the consolidation movement in the Philadelphia-area market and recognized the urgency to secure a strategic partnership or risk being marginalized.

When Rodger assumed the leadership, he inherited these conversations with Frank. The discussions, once tentative and exploratory, became progressively more substantive under his deft leadership, culminating in the acquisition: a monumental $1 billion deal finalized in 2022. This propelled WSFS' assets from $13 billion to $20 billion; significantly expanded our footprint into Philadelphia's prestigious Main Line suburbs; and, most importantly, enhanced our wealth management capabilities with Bryn Mawr's substantial portfolio, management talent, and reputation that extended to Wall Street and nationwide. Together, we managed or administered over $80 billion in other people's money: one of the largest bank-run wealth management operations in the US.

This acquisition, emblematic of the strategic foresight that has defined our approach, demonstrates one of my favorite adages: "Opportunities are multiplied as they are seized." Each step—Christiana, Array, Alliance, Penn Liberty, and Powder-mill—was not merely a business transaction, but a piece of a larger mosaic. Without these earlier, smaller acquisitions, Beneficial would have remained an unattainable prize. And without Beneficial, the opportunity to partner with Bryn Mawr Trust would not have been possible.

The WSFS Way

In the world of corporate mergers and acquisitions, the atmosphere is charged with uncertainty and stress. Direction can feel like it's constantly in flux; job cuts hang like a dark cloud; and it's easy for rumors, frustration, and discontent to take root.

At WSFS, we prided ourselves on doing things differently. We built our entire strategy around hyper-engaging our workforce, which included respecting people and treating them with great fairness and generosity, especially during separations.

We believed in clear and open communication around job changes. We promised our employees, "As soon as we know, we'll let you know." We gave six months' notice to anyone facing layoffs. Anybody who would be displaced in the merger had the first pick of other internal jobs, and always over applicants from the outside. For those few people we couldn't accommodate with our growth, we tried to provide as generous a severance package as possible—often going above what was in their company's original policy. We resolved to more than live up to our promises with our new partners: whether contractual, spoken, or implied.

This approach turned out to be a tremendous positive. Our new team members felt valued, trusted us, and were more inclined to get quickly and fully on board with the new organization. The broader business community also noticed our methods, and word spread that we were committed to doing the right thing.

Here's something that many organizations don't always do well, and at their own peril: communication. Through acquisitions, you need frequent, transparent communication; it must be routine and empathetic. We built integration teams with members from both the acquiring and acquired companies, people who helped ensure that decisions were wise, and updates were consistent and human. If reductions were necessary, we communicated them forthrightly, and well in advance. We treated everyone with respect. We documented successes *and* areas for improvement, conducting after-action reviews with all sides of the transaction. As we learned, we never stopped adjusting and enhancing our ongoing M&A "playbook."

At WSFS, our most cherished asset is our people, and we strived to maintain a workplace where they were eager to come to work, and work hard every day. Even during our intense acquisition phase, we earned the *Wilmington News Journal's* distinction of being a top workplace for 11 consecutive years. This recognition affirmed that our core values remained strong despite rapid growth. Our culture was, and always would be, our secret ingredient.

We were also fortunate to have a highly talented, acquisition-oriented CFO during these big deals and growth years. Dominic Canuso, who came to us through Barclays Bank, was a team player, and always well on top of deal analysis, due diligence, contracts, integration, and optimizing cost saves. We were doubly fortunate to be blessed with great advisors in M&A and capital transactions that were trustworthy, dogged experts, and knew how we liked to do things. Jimmy Dunne and Brian Sterling at Piper Sandler, along with Rusty Conner and Michael Reed at Covington & Burling, were with us through thick and thin over 25 years, and undoubtedly made us more successful in these endeavors.

Advice on Mergers and Acquisitions

1. Seek to combine companies that are in a related or synergistic business. Start small, grow organizational competency, then pursue acquisitions in increasing size and complexity.

2. Make sure they have compatible cultures and leadership styles, or that the acquired company can be easily molded.

3. From the outset, ensure there is a clear and cohesive post-merger strategy, leadership, and governance that's understood and communicated frequently.

4. Perform thorough, but not exhaustive, due diligence meant to uncover deal killers, deal changers, unknown risks, and opportunities to plan for in integration. Use top-notch, trusted advisors, counsel, and consultants.

5. Set proper pricing to ensure value creation that inures to BOTH seller and buyer.

6. Take a whiteboard approach to your vision for the new organization. If you were building from scratch, what would your company need to look like for the future?

7. Identify cost savings that are clear, quickly attainable, tracked, and that don't ruin the reason for the acquisition; some savings should be earmarked for investment in stronger infrastructure and revenue growth areas of the new, larger organization.

8. Build a dedicated integration team(s) with staff members from the buyer *and* seller, and outside experts.

9. Make sure integration communications are regular, transparent, and human—both inside and outside the organization.

10. When there are reductions in force, make sure they are communicated well, and well in advance. Treat separated individuals generously, and with dignity.

11. Throughout the process, document the things you did, did well, did not-so-well; conduct after-action reviews with members from all sides of the transaction including the buyer, seller, and advisors; and continually enhance your ongoing "playbook" for M&A.

NINETEEN | THE NEXT CHAPTER

By Mark Turner

"TRANSFORM."
This single word emblazoned on the title page of WSFS' 2018 annual report, released in early 2019, perfectly encapsulated the prevailing sentiment within the company.

For me, it was a moment of immense pride, just as I concluded my final year as CEO at a company I had seen through many transformations. The report marked this transition clearly—Rodger's photo now graced the "Letter from Management" page, signaling his takeover of my role. While I would remain as executive chair of the board, Rodger was firmly at the helm and his vision was clear:

I am committed to leading our Company to new levels of performance that will deliver sustained and premium returns for our Owners, and continued positive outcomes for all our Stakeholders, he wrote. *The best days of WSFS lie ahead and I look forward to leading this journey with all of you.*

At this point, my role was to support Rodger, assist the board with the transition, and continue to be an ambassador for the organization. Our investments were blossoming, and we were achieving some of the highest returns in the industry, and in our history: a notable ROA of 1.63 percent, and a 20 percent return on equity. While changes in the tax code contributed, our ongoing fundamental business growth in fee income, deposits, and loans was the main driver.

Our name recognition was also expanding rapidly throughout new communities, from southern Delaware to northern Delaware; southeastern Pennsylvania all the way to South Jersey and bustling Philly; and even nationwide with our wealth, leasing, and ATM businesses.

As I neared the end of my tenure at WSFS, I reflected on our journey. The strategy we developed in the early 2000s had indeed carried us through two decades of evolution. Through crises and uncertainties, we steadily pursued our goals—growing organically, one valued associate and one loyal customer at a time. Eventually, that had led to the company's ability and confidence to grow in big chunks through thoughtful, strategic partnerships and acquisitions. This is why I'm so passionate about the steadfast commitment to strategy, culture, and team: When in harmony, they are incredibly powerful, and lead not just to singular achievements, but to sustained excellence.

Over those 25-plus years, we transformed from a less than $2 billion bank with a challenging recent past to a $20 billion asset and local powerhouse. Our revenues and profit grew 20 times, and our market value grew 30 times, all while outperforming peer and broad index shareholder returns by many times over. Those numbers were once the stuff of fairytales for our small, community-focused bank. It was safe to say that the future had bright potential, but we vowed to never become complacent. There would always be room to grow and improve.

TWENTY | RISING INTO LEADERSHIP

By Rodger Levenson, as told to Brittany Kriegstein.
Rodger joined WSFS in 2006 as head of the Commercial
Lending department, and rose through the ranks to
become Mark's successor.

Starting back when I was chief commercial banking officer, Mark and I held weekly one-on-one meetings at PureBread, the coffee shop at the base of our headquarters on Delaware Avenue. My agenda typically revolved around issues within my team that needed attention. Then, one morning in 2013, Mark abruptly shifted the conversation. "I want to let you know I've been working on a plan," he said. "I've been discussing it with the board, and I intend to retire five years from now." He was clear: December 31, 2018, would be his last day as CEO. "This could open up some great opportunities for you," he added, "and while we don't have to address it right away, I wanted you to be aware."

I was taken aback, completely stunned by the news.

Mark explained his reasoning—he wanted to embark on a new chapter in life and believed having a structured plan was best for both himself and the bank. "How many companies do you see where the CEO leaves and they have no succession plan?"

I understood, but it was still shocking. I remember calling my wife, Julie, and blurting out, "You're not going to believe the conversation I just had with Mark."

Not in the Cards

When I joined WSFS in November 2006, becoming CEO wasn't on my radar. At that point, Mark was transitioning into the job, taking over the reins from Skip, and I came to see myself as Mark's partner and deputy. I was 45, and my wife and I had just had our first child. I was perfectly content as the number two, getting things done.

From the get-go, Mark felt like a guy I was going to work with for a long time, maybe even for the rest of my career. He had a clear vision for where he wanted to take the company and how he was going to do it, and we hit it off personally and professionally. I put in the time those first two years, forging a strong relationship with Mark while also working hard to build trust with my own team in the Commercial Lending department.

Then the financial crisis hit, followed by the Great Recession. It was an unprecedented economic shock. We knew it would be tough, but the pace of corporate collapses was staggering. Mark remained calm and composed despite the daily pressures, communicating our challenges and opportunities clearly. He reminded us to take things one day at a time, even as we faced daunting obstacles.

I stood by him, doing everything I could to help guide WSFS through that vulnerable period. But even as things began to stabilize, I didn't see a clear path to the top leadership role. Skip and Mark had set a high standard, and I had been sitting at the board table with them for years. Those were huge shoes to fill, and I wasn't sure I was the right fit.

But Mark was adamant in his confidence in me. The more I thought about it, the more I realized this could be a once-in-a-lifetime opportunity. His five-year timeline meant I would have a long lead time, with him mentoring me along the way. I began spending more time with Mark and Skip; observing, listening, learning, and imagining how this could unfold.

When the previous CFO left, I took on that role for 16 months, gaining valuable insights into that side of the business. I also became more involved in corporate development and acquisitions. About a year or two into Mark's plan, he approached me again, asking how I felt about the future. "You need to let us know if you're all in."

I said yes, I was. I was ready to commit.

Board Approval

No matter how much I prepared, though, the ultimate decision would be up to the board—which, at the time, wasn't particularly cohesive or functioning well as a team. And there were members who weren't happy that Mark had decided to take succession matters into his own hands; something that Mark admits he didn't handle well. There were questions about my readiness, about whether they should conduct an external search, and if I should be included in that process. Mark did an excellent job of shielding me from that tension—I was completely unaware of it at the time. He kept things close to the vest, because I think he rightly didn't want to reveal what was going on behind closed doors.

Not long afterward, Mark headed out on his Leading Practices Tour, and I stepped up to the plate. Thankfully, his time away coincided with a manageable period—nothing like the financial crisis tumult. It was really an opportunity for me to show the board and the team my style, up close and personal.

Still, we were busy: In late 2016, WSFS was signing or closing three acquisitions (Penn Liberty Bank, West Capital Management, and Powdermill Financial Solutions) and dealing with the industry fallout of the Wells Fargo incident (though it only had a modest impact on WSFS). There was also turnover on the board, and the day-to-day events that I needed to deal with.

I kept all the balls in the air and tried to channel Mark's quiet strength whenever things got challenging. And as the months went on, board members came around. In August 2017, I was elevated to COO, a key signal that I was second in command and, if I performed, would likely be Mark's successor.

Still, things were far from settled. It was a very rigorous process. Besides my internal training, I participated in a slew of external development programs, including a week at the Center for Creative Leadership in Boulder, Colorado—which included two half-day coaching sessions, a public speaking session, and crisis-management communication workshops.

Then there were multiple interviews with board members and executives, both one-on-one and in groups. An intensive, 360-degree review, with feedback from several board directors, was part of that process.

As I sharpened my skills and embraced the COO role, Mark was never out of reach. If I was at the head of the table, Mark was in the back making comments if needed. And every Tuesday morning at seven o'clock, we still had our one-on-ones, when I would bring my familiar legal pad of problems and discussion points that I'd written out the night before. But one day, I remember that Mark told me to put away the legal pad. Instead, he asked: "What are you doing to take care of yourself? Are you getting enough sleep? You know how important sleep and exercise are. How's your family doing?"

Mark had this great way of touching base when you least expected it, even on a personal level. We had a lot of important stuff to talk about that morning, but we didn't end up talking about it. From his own experiences and mistakes, he knew how crucial it was for me to have a good balance in life.

Outside of our halls, Mark was also taking me around, introducing me to key partners and ensuring that the bank's stakeholders would experience a seamless transfer of power. The transition, like almost everything Mark does, was well thought-out, planned, and structured, which benefited us all. I've seen so many people coast once they set their retirement date. Not Mark.

After I officially took the reins on January 1, 2019, he was still helping me develop—checking in periodically from his role on the board. As prepared as I now felt for the job, I knew I'd have to strive every day to match his integrity and work ethic. Even when he wasn't directly in charge anymore, he was still pushing all of us to be the best we could be.

Unprecedented Times

Not long into my time as CEO, the unthinkable happened: a global pandemic. The whole world closed down in March of 2020, leaving everyone scared and anxious. Unlike other crises that had rocked the banking industry, this wasn't just a bunch of bad loans. This was an existential event that was affecting life as we knew it. We had no playbook, no guide.

Thankfully, Mark was still on the WSFS board, and was a real lighthouse for me in the face of dark, uncertain waters. Of course, he didn't have all the answers about what would happen. But he did have some crucial advice: "Think through things, come up with a plan, be very structured, and over-communicate." At that time of extreme unpredictability, people needed a source of solid routine. It was Mark's idea for me to provide an update for the company every day at 4:00 p.m.—even if there was nothing especially noteworthy to say.

There were other important factors that helped us get through the pandemic in a position of strength. One, of course, was the strong culture we'd worked so hard to build during Mark's tenure. Another was the diversity of our products and investments, and the opportunities we'd boldly seized. A third advantage was our digital platforms—which we'd poured so much effort into long before the world became a bunch of Zoom meetings and online services. And the fourth? The fact that we'd been around for almost 200 years, doing our best to serve our community.

There's a major responsibility that comes with being around for so long. In almost two centuries, Mark was only the 12th CEO; I'm just the 13th. This company has endured wars, recessions, pandemics, banking crises, depressions, and so much more. As the current leader, it's up to me to keep us going through whatever lies ahead.

Mark knew exactly how that felt, and I did call him often during those uncertain pandemic days. Though he usually knew the right thing to do, he never prescribed it. He steered me towards getting on the right path in his quiet, steady way. I can never thank him enough.

TWENTY-ONE | THE QUIET END OF AN ERA

By Mark Turner

My last day as CEO at the place I'd called home for more than two decades was remarkable in that it wasn't. There was no fanfare, no drama, no tears, or surprises. It was also fairly anticlimactic because my last day happened to be December 31, 2018, which was in the middle of the quiet holiday period. But my last day and Rodger's first day were thoughtfully planned to be just like any other—and that's the lesson here.

When everyone came back to work on January 2, 2019, Rodger had officially taken the helm, and the atmosphere at the bank was business as usual. The board and I had agreed that I would stay on as executive chair for about a year after my last day as CEO, to aid them and Rodger in the transition to new leadership. Rodger had already worked for WSFS in senior leadership positions for many years, and he was more seasoned than I'd been when taking on the CEO role, so it was an easy process. I was able to increasingly fade into the background as a non-executive board member for the following years until my planned, full retirement from WSFS in 2022.

The lack of drama was a key indicator that our very deliberate succession plan had worked. Only small changes were noticeable to outsiders. I no longer had an office in our main headquarters because I didn't want to be in Rodger's way. Instead, I asked to set up a small, remote office at our Greenville, Delaware center where I could keep up with my continued work as executive chair. I wouldn't be attending any internal meetings; my main roles that year were to help guide and mentor Rodger, to make sure the board acclimated to Rodger's leadership style, and to otherwise be a good ambassador for the organization.

My real last day with WSFS was in April 2022, when I had my final board meeting. That milestone was marked by a few celebratory activities: My team had taken me out to dinner, and Peggy and I reminisced one day over a martini in my office—a nod to one of our long-standing jokes about not being able to "drink on the job" anymore. The company ran full-page ads in local newspapers about my departure, thanking me and wishing me well on a new chapter in my life.

The night after that last board meeting, the board members and my team threw me a going away party at the Mark A. Turner Innovation Center—a new suite dedicated to my time at WSFS, located in our new building at 1818 Market Street in Philly. We had recently acquired Beneficial Bank; and with it, their building; which we refurbished to be a second headquarters. The MAT Center, fittingly, was designed to be a place of teamwork, collaboration, and learning; with photos, videos, and some of my favorite quotes on the walls. It was right then that we were commemorating my work at WSFS in my hometown, while also celebrating an acquisition that had propelled us to be the largest bank headquartered in the region.

The event was a tremendously warm send-off, attended by a slew of board members, associates, executives, management, and many of their spouses. Skip and CG made touching speeches; the room was decorated with photos that captured key moments of my tenure. Ted couldn't be there in person, but he sent Skip some moving remarks to make on his behalf. CG has never been effusive with praise, so I'll never forget when he said, "Skip took us to the elites of 'college banking,' and Mark took us to the pros." As you might guess, this was right after college basketball's March Madness had wrapped up.

On my end, there was no regret, and there were no sad feelings. This transition was well-planned, and well-executed. I guess the emotions had played out over several years, so I was left with a profound sense of warmth and accomplishment. In 25 years, we went from a small, scrappy, third-rate company to a premier regional organization, the model of sustained excellence and strong culture that was rated a top workplace for many years running. The numbers also tell the story. That "10, 20, 30" growth and outperformance took a group of smart, dedicated, and creative teammates; all rowing in the same direction; it took a focused, differentiated strategy; and a robust culture, all working together.

It felt strange to be leaving, but it also felt right. I'd done everything I could for WSFS, and the bank had done the same for me—giving me an extraordinary career; a vocation, really; and the chance to work with some incredible people. My daughters Becky and Katie were growing into amazing young women, and I wanted to spend more time with them and Regina before the girls left the nest. I also wanted to pursue other opportunities.

As under Skip's tenure, WSFS rose through exceedingly difficult challenges and surmounted what at times seemed insurmountable. From there, we nurtured our communities and created sustainable excellence at a company that had once seemed doomed to fail. Every generation should get better and serve as the springboard for the next, and Rodger and his team are the right people to lead the company to even greater success.

We got to the upper echelon in what I believe is the right way: our associates, customers, business partners, investors, and communities benefited from our growth and success, and we from theirs. Because of that, they were pulling for us, and we for them. Real, sustainable success is about that web of connection and mutual support—the *and*, not the *or*. Strategy *and* culture must be united, it's not one *or* the other. It's about *all* of the constituents winning, not setting shareholders' interests *against* other stakeholders' interests. It's about making the pie bigger for everyone to enjoy.

APPENDIX I | LESSONS LEARNED THAT WORK

Gleaned over many years of experience and observation; most are exemplified throughout this book, and many of the below can fall into more than one category.

On Leadership

1. True leadership is building a network of mutually reinforcing constituents that create a flywheel of virtuous and long-term success. In business, have as a goal that your associates, customers, business partners, investors, and communities all benefit from your growth and success, and you from theirs. If so, they will help you and pull for you, and you for them, in good times and bad. It's about *all* of the constituents winning; not, for example, setting shareholders' interests *against* stakeholders' interests. Make the pie bigger and richer for everyone.

2. Similarly, your personal success in business (and life) is the residual of your commitment to the success of others—associates, customers, shareholders, business partners, friends, and family. The residual starts as a trickle but, over time, turns into a flow.

3. The foundational work of a leader is to build and enhance trust with all constituents over time. Most leadership failures happen because trust is lost with a key constituent. Many businesses are sold because the CEO loses the trust of the board, which is usually preceded by the CEO's loss of trust with associates, regulators, shareholders, etc.

4. The job of a CEO during "normal" times is to be an ambassador of the organization to those *outside* the walls of the headquarters. Visit with your associates, customers, business partners, competitors, and community. Show confidence, authenticity, and humility. Bring the best of the inside to them, and the best of the outside back into the organization.

5. The critical work of a CEO during crisis time is to maintain a clear head, a steady hand, to adhere to your values, set a temporary new course, take action, be seen, build trust, enlist all your constituents in the task, and communicate often with a mix of realism and hope.

6. Be the best version of your authentic self, and always be working on that best version. The best version includes being human, real, and humble. Quote, "If you want to impress someone, tell them about your successes; if you want to improve someone, tell them about your failures." Look to improve others much more than you impress them. That will make the most lasting impression.

7. Be open and transparent, but not every concern in your head needs to be shared. Become practiced at the art of "managed transparency."

8. Be responsible, reliable, live up to and exceed promises—those that are contractual, spoken, and implied. Be there for people, and don't disappoint when you can possibly avoid it.

9. The difference between good managers and good leaders? "Good managers do things right; good leaders do the right things."

On Strategy

1. Strategy is the relentless focus on two things: being different, and being excellent at that difference. Be different in what you provide, how you provide it, or both. Even commodities can be made special and worth a premium. Then, be excellent, or "uncatchably first," at that difference. Everything you do should be synergistic, and enhance and reinforce the main thrust of your business to make it lasting, and nearly impossible to copy.

2. Your strategic plan should be set out in a shared document, which must be concise, clear, different, memorable, accessible, and "you." Everyone in the organization (from new associates to board members) should have the opportunity to participate in the planning process, and they should be able to "see themselves" in the plan. A strategic plan is not really effective unless it changes behaviors at every level of the organization on a daily basis.

3. A critical skill in effecting strategy is the ability to say no quickly to many things that don't fit or distract, so you can focus on the few things you should be saying yes to.

4. Concentrations kill. Diversify revenue, resources, and risk. Many organizations fail because of an overexposure to a small number of customers, one business segment, one business partner, one location, or one leader. The concentration may not appear risky, but it can be deadly.

5. Always be asking not just what customers need, want, or will want; but what they are willing to pay a premium for. Think Starbucks for coffee and Apple for phones.

6. Always be looking ahead and around the corner. Get out of the office and visit with associates, customers, competitors, owners, and practice leaders to find out what's next. Disrupt yourself before you get disrupted. Be your own activist.

7. Prove that your organic growth works before pursuing acquisition growth. Before you grow in chunks by buying market share, make sure you have something customers want and will pay a premium for; i.e., something that is worth growing.

8. Embrace the value of optionality in taking on new things. They may prove fruitful in and of themselves, but also by what other opportunities they attract. "Opportunities are multiplied as they are seized."

9. Treat regulation and good regulatory stature/relations as a strategic advantage. Earning the trust of your regulator will give you more opportunities to expand your business in good times, and keep you out of the doghouse in tough times. Good stature will allow management to stay in charge of its business decisions. This will allow you to outperform competition that doesn't take a similar approach.

On Team

1. The goal for CEOs (and executives) is to become a "Leader of Leaders." Develop the leadership abilities of the team and allow them to lead—which will multiply your leadership to cover the entire organization; now, and for the next generation.

2. Develop a direct-reports team that is full of eights and nines (out of 10), but come together and operate as an 11. Pick members carefully for their complementary skills: enthusiasm for teamwork and desire for the greater good. Instill global goals and incentives, and recognize and reward selflessness. Tens have their place in sole contributor roles, but be cautious about placing superstars in teams, as they can be self-absorbed and disruptive.

3. Make "Talentship" the first and most important agenda item at strategic off-site meetings. Each executive should report on, and be accountable for, their unit's succession planning, bench-strength building, and development plans for top performers and up-and-comers.

4. Use difficult projects and crisis times to identify those who will rise to more responsibility, and those who will shrink from it. Invest in the risers, and remediate or separate them from the shrinkers.

5. Occasionally, and strategically, be silent or completely absent in your own organization. Allow others to speak up and rise up to reveal themselves and their potential.

6. Having a management team that is too strong for the board, or a board that is too strong for management, are both bad situations. Strive to have a board and executive management team that are equally strong, and constantly raising the bar on each other. (See separate appendix on successful boards).

On Execution

1. Follow the 80 percent rule on decisions: Be very comfortable making big decisions with only 80 percent of the information. The last 20 percent will be unclear and take too long to get, and the opportunity will be gone. Mitigate the huge downsides of big decisions, though the only way to really know what you've got is to own it, then determine the real situation and make it work.

2. When making big decisions, designate a "miner of conflict"—a contrarian voice who will be charged with raising possible doubts, questions, and challenges to the rest of the group. It is a healthy deterrent/preventative to "group think," and ensures that all points of view and comments are heard without causing ill will among the team.

3. Focus on the capabilities and track record of the management team. If properly vetted, all ideas that make it through will have merit. It's the management team that will make them go, or not.

4. The CEO is the organization's primary risk manager—the one person who knows all the facets of the organization, its strategies, internal and external contexts, the risks it actively takes, and its capabilities. The CEO must be the architect and overseer of the enterprise-wide risk management system; and with the board and good counsel, the one who handles making all the big, risky decisions.

5. The antidote for anxiety and uncertainty is action. Organizations and people can be paralyzed by those two emotions. The best remedy is to take action—starting small, which helps build momentum to tackle the big challenges. That moves people in a positive direction, sets their mind on the constructive, inspires confidence, relieves the overwhelmed feeling, and gets things done.

6. Leadership, governance, strategy, and culture during acquisitions must be strong, simple, and clear. When combining, from the outset, one CEO, one leadership team, one board, one culture, and one business model must be dominant. It can be a melding of people and processes from both organizations, but the leadership and direction must be clear to avoid conflict, confusion, wasting time, and opportunities. (See separate appendix on advice on mergers and acquisitions.)

7. Remember, "Whoever gets to the truth first, wins." Great input and ideas can come from anywhere. When things go wrong, don't engage in finger pointing and punishment; rather, focus on learning the lesson, holding people professionally accountable, and moving forward.

8. Second chances: People do make and should make mistakes. As an organization, when determining whether to take a chance on someone who has failed, big time, ask: "Is this person's potential worth the risk?" "Do they acknowledge their part in the bad situation?" "Can they genuinely articulate what they would do differently next time?" "Do they have foundational character to grow through their failures?" If so, they will likely be a better professional for you, and more motivated to prove themselves. Don't discard people when they are at a big inflection point of learning, growth, and productivity.

9. In every crisis there are problems and opportunities. Part of the organization should deal with the problems, while another should be fully dedicated to the learnings and opportunities. Remind the team, "Every cloud has a silver lining; If you can't see it, find it; if you can't find it, make it." Optimize whatever situation you have in front of you.

10. Get into work an hour before the day starts. Clear your desk, your mail, your head. Read and prepare. Prioritize the day. Most importantly, get in the right mindset to be successful that day. Be fully ready when the action begins.

On Communication

1. Bring mindset before skillset. Skillsets are greatly enhanced when preceded by a good mindset (and are greatly diminished with the wrong mindset). Before every meeting, every important interaction, think, "What attitude is needed for me to be most helpful to them?" When building a daily to-do list, put alongside it, "Who do I genuinely need 'to be' to best accomplish this?"

2. Public speaking mindset: Prepare and approach it as a comfortable conversation about a topic you are both passionate about, and authoritative on. Avoid trying to be perfect for you. Rather, focus on being effective for them, the audience.

3. Public speaking guide: Only agree to speak when you are passionate about the topic. If your passion is not apparent, first try to find an angle in the topic that excites you; if you can't, find someone else who is passionate to do the communicating. As a leader, people will want to hear from you often. It's OK to say "no" to a request, but try to offer a better alternative.

On Culture

1. Get strategy, culture, and team to unite. At WSFS, "We Stand For Service" was both our strategy and our culture. We strove to be the best bank for service anywhere, and our top values were we "serve others" and "do the right thing." Our team was built around the same values.

2. Continually stress your mission and values—the "why" and "how" of your existence. Over time, you will attract like-minded, talented, passionate associates; customers; and partners who want to work with you and support your "why" in the right way. Doing that will also make it very clear which associates, customers, and partners will *not* fit with your purpose and values, and they will go elsewhere. Both will make you an organization of integrity, strength, and longevity.

3. To enhance culture: Work it daily—top-down, bottom-up. Leaders have to believe in, and exemplify, culture all the time. Tie all important moments in an organization's life to your strategy and values. Find and tell stories that become cultural folklore. Everyone in the organization should be responsible for action plans to improve their work environment that are consistent with company goals and values. Culture should not be treated as a project or one group's responsibility; rather, it's a shared passion that brings life and purpose to the organization, and to every associate.

4. Make culture your organizational "immune system"—one that quickly spots offending people, behaviors, policies, practices, etc.; and deals with them before they can really harm the organization.

5. When you must separate with good people, whether through mergers, restructurings, downsizings, even performance, be overly fair and treat them with dignity. As a human being, they deserve it; and the rest of the organization is watching and will take note of how you treat people during their most vulnerable times, and your position of leverage. When you do it well, over time, the whole organization will be more secure, more dedicated, more productive, and more willing to take good risks.

6. Your organization's values are a paradox: both true and aspirational. Stress that you need to get better at "who we are" and "how we behave," every day.

APPENDIX II | PRINCIPLES FOR A SUCCESSFUL BOARD

1. Recognize that, with management, the board is the organization's most important team. Board members select, motivate, and hold the CEO accountable to execute the mission and strategy according to the organization's values. The board also sets the tone of "Do/Do Not" within the organization—helping put the guardrails in for growth, innovation, and risk-taking.

2. Get to the right number. The most effective and most efficient boards generally have 8–12 people. These are also the ones members feel provide the best experience and most fulfillment. The board should be as small as possible to get all the work done with the right balance of expert and diverse voices. No one hides, everyone contributes. This enables strong, nimble, united decision-making.

3. Get to the right composition. Match members' expertise to the strategic plan. Make sure there is a diversity of skills, experience, backgrounds, and constituent representation. Adhere to the tenure rule of thirds: approximately one-third of members with 1–5 years on the board, one-third with 5–10 years, and another third with 10–15 years. Be careful not to have too many retirees, lawyers, "celebrities," or ex-CEOs.

4. Create a good social contract—and continually self-police. Stress that this is a serious job. Every seat is valuable. Board members are not members for life. At the table, members should be prepared to contribute; they should be collegial, constructive and speak and vote with their conscience. There is no need for term limits or age limits, as members must continually earn their seat.

5. Partner with management. Boards are at risk of having a strength and power imbalance with management. The goal should be to have each entity equally strong, and continually pushing each other to be better. Executive sessions of the board should be regular but restrained—avoid having two meetings where the agenda meeting is followed by the "real meeting" in an executive session. All meaningful discussions should take place in the boardroom, and with management present if at all possible; resist heavy sidebars and member cliques.

6. There should be a strong chair (and committee chairs). The chairs should set the tone of board members working with each other and with management, ensuring that the board stays in the governance lane. They should work with the CEO to set the agenda; they should guide discussions; regulate the over-voiced and encourage the under-voiced members; and bring items to a quick, clear conclusion—or table items for later discussion. After appropriate analysis and discussion, they should seek decisions with buy-in, not necessarily unanimity. They should plan for crises and outside pressures, and set the tone for how to handle them.

7. Create an environment of constructive challenge and team-work. Board members should both support and challenge management as the situation merits—asking questions until they're satisfied. Big items should be reviewed at least twice before everyone votes. Stress that it's OK to vote "no," but no one should abstain (except in cases of conflict of interest). Dinners and off-sites are necessary for relationship building and group bonding.

8. Maximize focus on the strategic; relegate the tactical. All heavy lifting should be done within the committees and presented to the full board to discuss and approve. Committee chairs should report out big items discussed to the full board at the following meeting. Short meeting pre-calls are helpful to prioritize topics and time, and to ensure that the materials needed to make an informed decision are present. Make generous use of a consent agenda for routine and administrative matters.

9. Plan for crisis and dilemmas. Tough moments will arise. Have a small, board "crisis team" ready with access to expert internal and external resources. Routinely "scenario plan" for problems. When a dilemma arises, ask the following three questions, in this order: 1) What is the right thing to do in accordance with our mission and values? 2) How can we create value out of this situation, regardless? 3) If a decision does not comport with public, press, or political sentiment, how do we explain it well and then stand by it?

10. Set processes for board self-improvement and refreshment. Implement post-meeting surveys with short, simple, questions which must be answered timely. There should be annual board self-assessments and gap analysis, with an outside expert/facilitator to help every three years. Comments should be synthesized, constructive, and not attributed to any one person. Curate an active pipeline and succession plan for the board as members are nearing the end of their tenures. Train board leadership skills using committee chair roles.

APPENDIX III | ADVICE ON MERGERS AND ACQUISITIONS

1. Seek to combine companies that are in a related or synergistic business. Start small, grow organizational competency, then pursue acquisitions in increasing size and complexity.

2. Make sure they have compatible cultures and leadership styles, or that the acquired company can be easily molded.

3. From the outset, ensure there is a clear and cohesive post-merger strategy, leadership, and governance that's understood and communicated frequently.

4. Perform thorough, but not exhaustive, due diligence meant to uncover deal killers, deal changers, unknown risks, and opportunities to plan for in integration. Use top-notch, trusted advisors, counsel, and consultants.

5. Set proper pricing to ensure value creation inures to BOTH seller and buyer.

6. Take a whiteboard approach to your vision for the new organization. If you were building from scratch, what does your company need to look like for the future?

7. Identify cost savings that are clear, quickly attainable, tracked, and that don't ruin the reason for the acquisition; some saving should be earmarked for investment in stronger infrastructure and revenue growth areas of the new, larger organization.

8. Build dedicated integration team(s) with members from the buyer, seller, and outside experts.

9. Make sure integration communications are regular, transparent, and human—both inside and outside the organization.

10. When there are reductions in force, make sure they are communicated well, and well in advance—treat separated individuals generously and with dignity.

11. Throughout the process, document the things you did, did well, did not-so-well; conduct after-action reviews with members from all sides of the transaction, including the buyer, seller, and advisors; and continually enhance your ongoing "playbook" for M&A.

ACKNOWLEDGMENTS

This book would not be here without the kind, patient, and skill-ful work of both my co-writers, Brittany Kriegstein and Lizzie Simon—and of course, all the people who supplied quotes and reflections in various chapters.

I also thank the many mentors, role models, and confidants over my professional years, especially Skip Schoenhals, Ted Weschler, CG Cheleden, Karl Johnston, Bill Abbott, Dale Wolf, J.J. Davis, Anat Bird, Cal Morgan, Steve Booth, Jacque Merritt, Laurisa Schutt, Irina Baranov, Jimmy Dunne, Mike Hughes, and John Broderick. They supported my growth, and much of what is in here I learned with and through them.

My classmates, teachers, and administrators at St. Joe's Prep, LaSalle, Wharton, the University of Nebraska, and the many advanced education institutes I attended were likewise instru-mental in my journey.

And thank you to all the current and past associates of WSFS, especially my dear, longtime teammates Skip, Rodger, and Peggy. You made an almost 200-year-old company continuously relevant, of great service to its communities, sustainably excellent, and made my small part in its storied history possible.

Last and most importantly, I thank my mom and dad, broth-ers and sisters, close relatives, friends, and especially my wonder-ful wife Regina and amazing daughters Becky and Katie for their guidance, support, and love through my lifetime. They make all the good things in this world achievable and worthwhile for me.

ABOUT THE AUTHORS

Mark Turner was born, raised, and schooled in North Philadelphia. He has spent the majority of his career in banking, primarily at WSFS Bank, where he held the roles of CFO, COO, CEO, and Executive Chair. A lifelong learner, he received degrees from LaSalle University, the University of Pennsylvania, and the University of Nebraska; and attended many executive education experiences in the decades thereafter. Today, he serves on boards, and guest lectures at universities and executive forums. Mark likes to run, golf, read, and travel. He and his brilliant wife, Regina, VMD, PhD, live in Chester County, Pennsylvania, and together have raised two amazing daughters, Becky and Katie.

Brittany Kriegstein is a journalist and writer based in New York City whose work has appeared in WNYC/*Gothamist*, *The New York Times*, *The New York Daily News*, *Business Insider*, *El Diario*, and more. She lives in Brooklyn with her fiancé, and covers news stories across all five boroughs. She previously helped Mark Turner's predecessor, Skip Schoenhals, with his book *From Failing to Phenomenal: The Story of WSFS from 1985–1996*.

Lizzie Simon is the author of the groundbreaking memoir, *Detour* (Atria Books). At *The Wall Street Journal*, she was a weekly arts columnist focusing on dance and theater. Lizzie is currently developing several television series, and working as a developmental editor and ghostwriter on a handful of memoirs-in-progress. You can find her popular weekly newsletter, Lizzie's Letter, on Substack. For more information, visit www.lizziesimon.info.

www.ingramcontent.com/pod-product-compliance
Lightning Source LLC
Chambersburg PA
CBHW021500180326
41458CB00051B/6895/J